LEADERSHIP CAFFEINE:

IDEAS TO ENERGIZE YOUR PROFESSIONAL DEVELOPMENT

ISBN-10: 1456493876
EAN-13: 9781456493875
LCCN: 2010919425

LEADERSHIP CAFFEINE:

IDEAS TO ENERGIZE YOUR PROFESSIONAL DEVELOPMENT

Slightly More than Eighty Power-Packed Essays on Improving Your Effectiveness as a Leader, Manager, Motivator

&

All-Around Great Professional!

⌘

Art Petty

Dedication:

To Allison, Kyle and Michael for putting up with my need to write
and
for serving as the inspiration.

To my Dad, Roger,
and
to the memory of my Mom, Carol,
for providing the foundation.

Contents

Section 9: In Pursuit of Greatness 273

Section 10: The Lighter Side of Leadership Caffeine 305

Preface

This collection of essays is for every professional, leader and manager interested in strengthening performance, doing right by their people and organizations and being true to themselves. If you fit this description, welcome! You're in the right place and it is my sincere hope that the ideas, experiences and suggestions included between these covers provide help, guidance and even a bit of inspiration for you as you navigate your professional journey.

I make no secret about my passion and mission for developing great leaders, great professionals and high performance teams. I work hard as an educator, coach and consultant, in pursuit of this mission, and this collection on leading, developing yourself, developing others, dealing with tough days, managing your boss and having a few laughs along the way, is just one small contribution. Creating this collection has been a labor of love for me over the past few years as I've worked with and learned from many remarkable individuals.

The content is largely drawn from my work at my Management Excellence blog, where I unabashedly try ideas on for size and develop my thoughts. Fortunately, a good number of readers are all too happy to help me see the errors of my way, and I'm able to keep refining and improving my work in real time.

And while regular blog readers will recognize many of these essays as, "posts," I can assure you this book is much more utilitarian in its layout, organization and structure, than trying to sort through some 650 (and growing) posts. Blogs are great…books, whether paper or in electronic format are better when there's a specific use in mind. Which brings me to my advice for getting the most out of this collection:

1. You can read it from cover to cover, but be forewarned that there's no specific plot, no detailed character development, no build-up, no climactic scene and no dénouement. It's a collection of idea prompting, best practices essays organized into discrete sections by topic for easy reference. You can try reading it in order, and if a story emerges, drop me a note!

2. I encourage you to reference the book when you are feeling challenged and overwhelmed, as well as during days when you feel like you are the King of the World. You will find an ample supply of ideas and motivation, and there's an equally rich supply of content to keep you grounded and focused on helping others. Use the section listings in the Table of Contents to find the topic that relates to your current issues and grab and consume an essay just like you might reach for that morning cup of caffeine or evening age-appropriate beverage. Like a cup of coffee, these things are intended to offer refreshment and energy in small doses.

3. Use my ideas and suggestions to prompt your own ideas. Much like building and jumping on ideas in brainstorming sessions, you should do the same here. And of course, remember to dog-ear pages, jot notes in the margins or use your e-reader to annotate and capture thoughts. It's easy to lose track of those important, fleeting ideas in the maelstrom of day-to-day activities.

4. Try and read at least one essay per week. Alternate sections every week. Put ideas to work and keep learning and refining them as you go. Do this consistently, and I'll guarantee that you will be a very different kind of professional fifty or so essays from now. Your team will notice the difference, you will notice the difference, and your family might even notice the difference.

The Bottom-Line for Now:

I'll end the preface as I do all of my essays, with a bottom-line. It's my goal to address and support the "difference-makers" in the world. The fact that you are here reading these words tells me that you are striving to be one of those who wants to make a difference for your firm, your team, your loved ones and for yourself. Thanks for taking me along on your journey. You'll do the heavy lifting, but it is my honor to provide support and occasional sustenance along the way.

— Art Petty at Crystal Lake, Illinois on this 21st day of May in 2011.

Prologue
The Great and Perilous Leadership Journey Ahead

I wrote this essay as a guest post for one of my favorite bloggers, Tanveer Naseer (www.tanveernaseer.com). I selected it to lead off the book because it provides critical context to all of us for the world we live and work in and the challenges we face as professionals and leaders. It's my polite form of a leadership manifesto and a blatant challenge to all of us to push forward in search of new ways to lead and manage in this perilous and exciting new world.

W hile there's much about leading others that remains consistent over time, the environment in which we lead changes constantly. For experienced and developing leaders, the emerging environment is likely to offer a Dickensian world filled with *Best of Times* opportunities and *Worst of Times* challenges. Now might be a good time to revise your thinking on your role as a leader and to begin cultivating the skills and experiences required for success during the exciting and perilous journey ahead.

In a career supporting the development of leaders, I've never witnessed an environment as complex and personally demanding as the one we've all been living through for the past few years. The macro-forces in our world, including globalization, sustainability, diversity, shifting demographics and the inexorable march of technology all are converging to create a "new normal" characterized by chaos, time-compression and constant disruption. Tomorrow's leader truly must be armed with "The Right Stuff," or, he or she is at risk of becoming global road kill.

Leadership-The Basic Building Blocks Never Go Out of Style:

Certain characteristics, attributes and behaviors of effective leaders are timeless, regardless of the prevailing environment. Every leadership book ever written (including mine) emphasizes the importance of the following ten items:

1. A positive character

2. The need to earn respect

3. A high degree of credibility

4. Genuine regard for the development of others

5. Confidence in the face of adversity and ambiguity

6. The ability to motivate and inspire

7. Comfort conducting tough discussions

8. A style that is perceived as authentic

9. A willingness to stand up and fight for the right issues

10. Command of the business

While these items are timeless, the supporting set of skills and attributes needed to effectively prosecute the role of the leader do change with the times and technologies. Recognize and build these skills and your world will be filled with opportunities. Ignore them and you will most definitely experience the *Worst of Times* side of this equation.

Welcome to the Leadership Blender-Speed, Ambiguity, Adaptability & Vector:

There are so many complex variables at work in our world today, that the level of predictability is almost nil. The days of long-range plans are dead, replaced by a mid-term vision and a series of short-term ideas and experiments. The practicing leader must be strategically and tactically nimble, able to quickly identify, select and execute upon opportunities in rapid succession.

Every military general understands that once the enemy is engaged, *the plan* is rendered obsolete. What endures, is the effort, discipline and learning gained during the process of planning. The difference is subtle but important. Nothing occurs in reality like it is specified on paper. However, those who spend the time training, planning and assessing risks and opportunities are prepared to cope with the sudden onset of battlefield or marketplace chaos and ambiguity.

The need for speed must be tempered by a need for vector (direction). Speed without vector is just random activity, and in a world characterized by increasingly scare resources, including time, random activity is potentially fatal. Unlike the historic role of the leader in choosing direction, the new leader's responsibility is all about developing teams capable of recognizing, pursuing and seizing emerging opportunities. You still get a big vote on key decisions, but, your primary role today is bringing the talent and tools to bear to help others recognize, conquer and then to move on in pursuit of the next opportunity.

A Critical New Skill-Set-Leading Without Authority:

In a world without traditional borders of time, geography and culture, the new leader must be capable of assembling and motivating temporary teams to seize opportunities. The goal is to bring the best resources available at the time to bear on a problem or an opportunity. A good number of the resources will have little formal accountability to the team leader, yet, they will be eminently accountable to the team for results.

Today's role of Project Manager comes the closest to resembling tomorrow's leader, although, the role is grossly under-positioned and narrowly defined in most organizations to serve as an absolute model. The next few years will see a merging of roles, where leaders will need to be great project managers and project managers will be required to hone leadership skills to succeed.

Teams will increasingly take responsibility for selecting their own leaders, with the sole criterion being, "Who is the best possible person to help us succeed?" While this may sound a bit socialistic, it is purely capitalistic, driven by the goal to succeed in the market and to strengthen the firm. An outcome of this "fitness for purpose" approach to team leader selection, will be the need for leaders to be comfortable and adaptable to a shifting role as leader one day and follower the next.

Building Coalitions for Fun and Profit:

Power and politics are often interpreted as dirty words and less than noble pursuits. Tomorrow's leaders will need to shed their inhibitions about the pursuit of power and focus on working across groups to cultivate respect, support the work of others and at key moments, gain the help and support of others to stem a problem or seize an opportunity. The most effective leaders will be the ones who drive results through others and in turn, support the needs of others to drive their own results. Instead of a backroom type game, coalition building will become foreground and your success will be a function of your ability to make things happen for others.

Redefining Diversity:

Tomorrow's leaders face the remarkable challenge of working constantly across cultures, geographies and time zones to drive projects, create coalitions and seize opportunities. A gentleman that I recently interviewed personifies this situation. He is a citizen of India working in the Midwestern

United States leading a global development team with representatives from 4 countries on the team. Of the ten team members, only three report to him directly. This type of a leadership situation did not exist a generation ago, and now it's increasingly the norm.

Your ability to acclimate to individual cultures and to engage effectively with your global team members will be a material part of your job. And while people are people, you most certainly will need to learn the nuances of motivating, communicating with, providing feedback to individuals that all respond to power in very different ways.

An additional challenge in this category will be the need to blend the generations to leverage the experience of the oldest workers with the perspectives of the youngest. Much of the planet is aging quickly, and given difficult economic circumstances, the older workers will remain involved in some form or fashion for years to come. They represent remarkable talent, particularly when connected with the youngest of our workforce. Learning to blend and lead these mixed age teams is just another critical challenge for tomorrow's leaders.

The Bottom-Line for Now:

What a great opportunity for those that thrive on change and that cultivate advanced interpersonal and political skills. You will still be accountable to those timeless building blocks outlined at the beginning of this essay. Ultimately, however, you will be evaluated on your ability to cope with and succeed in an environment where the only constant is something representing nearly incomprehensible change. Enjoy this leadership journey of a lifetime, and remember to lead with honor, integrity and professionalism while helping others navigate the challenges along the way.

Section 1

Developing Yourself

L ong gone are the days when someone went to work for a business early in their career, only to emerge a few decades later into a modest but comfortable retirement. While there are some great companies committed to helping grow great people, there's also a clear understanding on everyone's part that nothing is forever. Or, at least there should be. As of this writing (2011), the economic unpleasantness of the past few years continues to roll through many sectors in our economy, and too many people have been caught unprepared as they suddenly face the need to reinvent their careers as part of their professional survival.

Given the global complexity and speed of change referenced in the prologue (The Great and Perilous Leadership Journey Ahead), things aren't going to get much easier for any of us in the years ahead. We either heed Peter Drucker's advice in his classic article, "Managing Oneself," or we risk becoming global road kill.

While this entire collection is focused on helping you strengthen your skills, this particular section emphasizes your distinct personal responsibility for managing your own development process. After all, if you don't, who will?

Chapter 1

What Does Your Professional Brand Say About You?

What do peers and managers perceive as unique about you in the workplace? What do you do so well, that people stop and take notice? What's your personal positioning strategy that meaningfully differentiates you from others in the minds of your customers, managers and stakeholders?

Y ou're to be excused if you need to reach for another cup of coffee while you contemplate these "brand called me" questions that you likely only think about once every two years when you update your résumé.

What is it about you and your approach to your career and work that sets you apart from the crowd in a meaningful and positive way? Successful professionals deliberately craft their professional positioning strategy and work hard at deliberately managing this strategy to grow their influence. While this may sound like so much marketing-speak to you, ignore the guidance at your own peril. Given the talent available in the marketplace as well as the need for firms to find and place the best and brightest in roles where they can help navigate the stormy seas of today's world, not having a professional positioning strategy is a commitment to floundering.

Six Tips for Developing Your Professional Positioning Strategy:

1. Know thyself: while this may be difficult depending on how far you are up the Emotional Intelligence ladder, I encourage you to seek out reliable feedback on how you are perceived and valued. One professional developed her own survey and asked peers, managers and team members to answer some direct questions on perceived contributions, strengths and weaknesses…anonymously, of course.

2. Assess the environment. A good strategist carefully considers environmental factors and forces, and so should you. Seek to understand your firm's strategic goals in the broader context of industry, market and global forces.

3. What does this external assessment potentially mean for you and for other employees? Is the firm placing increased emphasis on certain skill sets like project management? Are the priorities on cultivating cross-cultural relationships with suppliers? Is the emphasis on identification of new revenue streams? Are departments and teams being challenged to innovate? What else is going on that might require me to invest in developing or strengthening my skills? Tuning in to your firm's needs and strategic direction allows you to frame your own positioning approach and supporting activities.

4. What's working for my coworkers? More questions: who's getting ahead and why? Who is earning the plum project assignments? Who earned the most recent promotions? Are they better at cultivating influence than you are?

5. Drop the sarcastic "they must have pictures" thoughts and look at these individuals as objectively as possible. If the boss thinks highly enough of your peers to provide them with new opportunities, more responsibilities and more rewards, they must be doing something right. How would you characterize their brands? Observe and learn.

4

6. What does all of the above mean for you and your brand? If you've been diligent in asking and answering the issues above, you've gained some nice raw content to begin framing your own professional strategy and personal positioning. Considering that most people aren't working or even thinking about their careers at this level of detail, you've got a unique opportunity.

Tying Things Together-Ask and Answer:

- Based on a clear understanding of my strengths and weaknesses and my firm's needs, where do I need to invest in developing myself?

- What's my brand identity? What do I want to change about this identity?

- What's my desired professional value proposition? Guidance: craft a forward looking statement that addresses the issues of why people should trust, value, refer and rely upon you.

- What actions can I take to strengthen my skills, earn the trust and confidence inherent in my professional value proposition statement and increase my visibility?

- How will I measure my progress and continue to gain feedback?

The Bottom-Line for Now:

If this sounds like a cross between a strategy engagement and a marketing plan development, you're spot on in your assessment. You can choose to let your career happen or you can deliberately manage your own personal professional brand and value proposition. The former relies upon chance and the latter helps you create opportunities. I opt for the proactive and forward-looking approach.

Chapter 2

Trust, Performance and Your Success

Much of who we are and what we do in our professional lives is built on an unstable foundation of trust. Trust is hard earned and those bestowing trust do so slowly, carefully and tentatively, all the while testing for reasons to pull back and guard this precious personal asset.

True trust is rare in the workplace. It's also critical for high performance.

A number of years ago, our then Board Chairman chastised our executive team for failing to live up to our potential, with the comment, "You people don't trust each other enough to succeed." I recall rankling at the comment. In reality, he was right. Ours was an outwardly collegial yet quietly toxic environment. Once the source of the toxin was removed, trust expanded enough to make some big bets and pull them off.

Toxicity trumps trust every time.

An individual characterized as "high potential" by all of her managers and the firm's executive team, lost her way on a number of poor performing and high visibility initiatives. Called in to diagnose the situation, it quickly became obvious that she wore her "high potential" label for everyone to see. Instead of feeling like they were rallying around a common cause on their project teams, the participants perceived they were playing supporting roles to promote High Potential's career. The projects floundered and failed.

When team trust takes a holiday, so does performance.

Somewhere on his climb up the ladder, this individual forgot how important others were to his success. He grew impatient with valued team members that would have benefitted from his good coaching, and he set them adrift. While there may have been performance justification for his decisions, the common view was that he failed to provide adequate support and due process. More importantly, these individuals had helped him in his earlier days, and there was an expectation that their trust and support would be repaid. The hard-earned trust of his early days was squandered by his perceived selfish handling of the situation. Trust, once broken, is rarely repaired.

The Bottom-Line for Now:

Building trust is an extreme activity. You cannot build trust unless you give trust, and the act is much like handing your heart and your hopes to someone else, firm in the belief that they will carefully handle these items and return them to you safely.

There are no "Top Ten" lists here for building trust with others and earning trust from others. You do this one interaction at a time, with people watching and noting whether your actions consistently match your words. Trust is the essence of your professional brand. Build it carefully and methodically, guard it fiercely and ensure that your actions for others and in support of your team and your business strengthen it constantly. Remember, trust once broken, is rarely repaired.

Chapter 3

Developing as a Senior Contributor

I regularly use the label "Senior Contributor" (SC) to reference a state of management maturity that tends to exist somewhere between upper mid-level management or senior knowledge worker and the executive layer. While the hierarchical comparison may be imperfect, it's an easy way for people to understand my intent with the phrase.

The SC is a professional manager or individual contributor on the brink of realizing executive qualifications. This individual displays effective formal and informal leadership skills, value-creating critical and strategic thinking abilities, credible executive presence and a strong operating and quality orientation.

The SC is an individual who, whether by design or by accident, has consistently been challenged to deal with complex and ambiguous business situations and has proven capable of rallying efforts, forming high performance teams, and facilitating results that create value for customers, improve operations and thump competitors. This is one super contributor!

While the SC sounds like a comic book super-hero graced with unique powers, you most definitely do not need to be from a planet with a red sun or have encountered a radioactive spider to lay claim to your own mask and cape. However, you do have to deliberately focus on developing and honing your skills to gain membership into this league of outstanding professionals.

Senior Contributors are Made, Not Born:

I've yet to meet a SC that wasn't personally and professionally driven to learn, grow, overcome weaknesses, develop talents and place himself/herself in challenging situations as part of the development process. While some people have natural gifts that lend themselves to certain situations, membership in this league is open to anyone willing to put the effort forth. However, not everyone has the Intestinal Fortitude (IF) to succeed.

Seven Suggestions for Developing as a Senior Contributor:

1. Look in the mirror and recognize that this battle to develop and excel is all up to you. Your firm doesn't owe you this and cannot train you on it, and you certainly won't achieve the level of SC through seniority and marking time.

2. Face your fears. Given my description of the SC above, almost everyone will have to face and overcome some areas of discomfort. Typically, the development of advanced communication and presentation skills (and the confidence behind the skills) is frightening for people to face. Ironically, presentation skills are the easiest to learn, practice and refine. Others, like critical and strategic thinking capabilities, require a conscious effort to rewire long-standing ways of thinking and acting.

3. Learn to adjust your altitude. SCs are capable of scaling heights from the big picture of market and industry forces and changing customer attitudes and perceptions to the nuances of process and operating improvements. As part of the "rewiring" or better yet, new wiring, emerging SCs must focus on connecting tasks to strategies and market forces and vice-versa. Take some mental Dramamine, because the altitude adjustments will be fast and furious.

4. Quit looking for easy answers. There is no training course that, once completed, will bestow upon you the certificate of Senior Contributor. There are many, many, many resources, experiences and opportunities to gain insights and hone skills, but there is no silver bullet, so quit looking for it.

5. Great managers and mentors are priceless. A good manager and/or a good mentor can help you along the way. A manager that is committed to supporting the development of her people understands how important it is to challenge and coach team members. A mentor offers the perspective and context of experience and can serve as a valuable navigator. For those of you that lack one or both (a good manager and a mentor), the bad manager can serve as inspiration. I long ago developed a mental list of "things never to do," when it was my day to lead.

6. Use your time wisely. Read, read and then read some more. From Harvard Business Review to Fast Company to historical biographies, you cannot spend enough time soaking up the teachings of successful people and those people who have experienced and persevered through remarkable hardship. Make certain that most of your reading takes place away from the business bookshelf and tends towards history, biography and even literature.

7. Adopt a personal quality improvement program. Just as Franklin and Jefferson diligently recorded their decisions and their daily progress and activities, find a way to begin recording your own actions. Set goals, monitor and measure progress and strive to improve.

The Bottom-Line for Now:

If you're a senior manager, you already know that you want high performers and SCs driving your organization. Are you doing everything you can to promote the development of these key professionals on your team?

As an aspiring professional, responsible for forging your own brand in a complex world over a career that will easily span 50 years, what are you doing to step it up? Turn off the television, back away from the urgent unimportant, learn to overcome your own natural resistance, and get on with the good and hard work of developing yourself!

Chapter 4

Prepare Your Mind to Conquer Presentation Anxiety

Few phrases are capable of sending shivers down a person's spine like, "Bob and Mary, plan on presenting your ideas at our next meeting." Except perhaps, "Bob and Mary, you are both on the agenda to present at the next Board of Directors meeting."

For some people, the seemingly golden opportunity to show and share is akin to receiving a prison sentence with no hope for parole.

Some View Speaking as Cruel and Unusual Punishment:

While never seeking to be cruel by inviting people to present their ideas, I've had people tell me (after the fact) that they basically shut down from the time they were "invited" until it was over. One individual volunteered that during the weeks leading up to the board presentation, he suffered from sleeplessness, grinding of teeth, loss of appetite, disengagement from family, feelings of excessive stress and finally, a rolling wave of panic attacks. Yikes! While he did a great job, that's not a desirable or sustainable process for anyone to have to deal with when it comes to preparing to deliver a presentation.

Most everyone would agree that the extreme fear of speaking in front of a group is not rational, yet, for those so afflicted, the fear is every bit as real as if the judge was handing down the sentence and offering the choice between execution and delivering the speech. Many people would hesitate on making that call. "Hmmm, if I choose the former, can I can skip the presentation?"

While part of me wants to say, "man up," or some other gender appropriate, much more politically correct phrase for "grow some," (oops), I can't. I consistently spend between ten and twenty hours per week in front of groups ranging from workshops to keynotes to classes, and my journey from something resembling the individual above to someone that truly loves and seeks out opportunities to engage an audience is all too fresh in my mind.

No amount of cajoling will help someone overcome his or her fear of speaking. This is an intensely personal foe that is difficult to wrestle to the ground and pin. While there is some oft-repeated and worthwhile advice, ranging from hiring a coach to joining organizations such as Toastmasters, I've observed that a good number of people have learned to manage their anxiety by focusing on preparing their minds.

Six Starter Ideas for Coping and Even Conquering Presentation Anxiety:

1. Learn from Ben Franklin. Draw a line down the center of a blank piece of paper and label the left "positives" and the right "negatives." Over the course of the next few days, jot down all of the good things that will accrue to you from developing your skills as a presenter as well as all of the negatives. Return to the list daily, add new ideas and cross off those that have no basis in reality. For example, "I'll be fired immediately" for whiffing on the presentation is not going to happen. Neither will you be bound, have an apple stuffed in your mouth and roasted over an open fire. And I've yet to fall through a trap door on a stage. The positive list will be much longer...much more rational and this is where you should focus your mind.

2. Turn your thinking around. Develop a fear of not overcoming this bogeyman. On another sheet of paper, create a list of all of the potentially negative things that will happen if you don't develop comfort in front of an audience. Think about an endless cycle of the horrible symptoms described above. Throw in career derailment, reduced earnings potential and an artificial cap on your ability to succeed. There are some really great reasons for developing as a speaker and some truly significant implications of shrinking from or shirking this developmental area.

3. Turn your thinking around, part 2. Reorient your perspective to turn developing as an effective and confident speaker into your mountain to climb. You've already established the negatives of not succeeding and the positives that accrue from conquering this Mt. Everest. It's time to turn this into an all-consuming goal. Whether you take your inspiration from watching "The Biggest Loser," (hey, nothing intended here) or Wimbledon or the Tour De France, make this your event to pursue.

4. Start with some easy practice runs to build confidence. There are nearly countless opportunities to start practicing in front of groups in your workplace or in your personal life. Each practice run is an important part of your conditioning. Set a goal for achieving one opportunity per week in fairly friendly surroundings. Focus initially on content that you know well or topics that you are passionate about. And make certain that you ask for constructive criticism. If you're not getting any good criticism, find someone else to practice with for future sessions.

5. Learn to plan your message. I never speak without having first created my message map on a single sheet of paper. Place your core message at the center, your supporting messages hang off the core and each supporting message is backed by evidence. Build your update from that template and you will be amazed how much easier this processes becomes. The preparation of a good message map means that you are not only ready to present in a clear and concise manner, you are also ready to field questions. The message map is absolutely my best speaking friend.

6. Say it with a smile. As part of your climb up Mt. Everest, learn to manage your emotions. A simple technique that will help you immediately and that will warm your audience, is to smile while you talk. Don't grin like an idiot, but show your warmth and emphasize the smile.

The Bottom-Line for Now:

My intent in this essay is to offer hope along with a few lifelines for everyone that suffers from Pre-Speaking Traumatic Stress Syndrome. This is real, and you can shrink from it, shirk it or find a way to shine. And while there's a lot more to do than what I outlined in this post, remember, these are lifelines to help you rein in and focus your emotions. Now, enjoy the training and start climbing. The benefits to you in your career are priceless.

Chapter 5

What the Boss Hears When You are Talking

I'm not quite certain if this post is a violation of the "Boss Code," much like that masked man on television who blatantly betrays magicians everywhere by showing us how magic tricks work. Nonetheless, here goes.

The Secret:

Every time you open your mouth around the boss, she learns something about you that may determine your fate, or at least your fate while you are working for her.

As people of experience, managers hear things during conversations that have nothing to do with the conversation but everything to do with how we view and value you as a professional.

There, the secret is out! We're carrying on two lines of thought when you engage us. We're appropriately staying in the moment and attempting to support your inquiry, while we are processing on the following:

- How complete of a thinker is this person?

- How strong are his critical thinking skills?

- Are her ideas creative?

- Has he thought through the issue from all directions?

- Are the solutions innovative?

- Is she a systems thinker, taking into account the impact of the situation/ solutions on other parts of our organization?

- Is he asking me to do his job for him?

- Is she pursuing a political agenda?

- Has he sought out the experts for help?

- Do I have confidence in this person?

- Is she as smart as I thought she was?

- Is this someone that can do more for us?

I could keep going, but by now, you get the idea.

Someone once asked me when I take the time to evaluate performance and my response was something to the effect of "During every conversation and in every meeting." I was pleased to see that I was in good company on this point when I read former GE Chairman, Jack Welch's book, *Winning,* and noted the following in his first of eight points describing what a leader does: *"Leaders relentlessly upgrade their team, using every encounter as an opportunity to evaluate, coach and build self-confidence."*

The Bottom-Line for Now:

Challenge yourself to develop your critical thinking skills. Think about the questions above and make certain that you are adept in scaling from the big picture to the details and agile enough to circle the issues. Remember to plan your messages and know that every encounter is an opportunity to showcase why you are worth investing in for the future. And remember, executives like "complete thinkers" that take every opportunity to solve even bigger problems for organizations.

Chapter 6

At Least 4 Additional Skills You Must Develop to Succeed

With the clear disclaimer that there are no magic formulas, silver bullets or guaranteed fast-track approaches to success in the workplace, there are a number of critical steps you can take to accelerate progress and improve your odds.

4 Key Areas You Must Develop to Succeed in Today's Workplace:

1. Learn to See Yourself as Others See You.
Short of having a genuine out-of-body experience, learning to see yourself as others see you is a challenging task. Our own view to our strengths and weaknesses is often inaccurate, based in large part on the fact that we're human.

Overcoming our own self-perception biases requires good outside help. I encourage emerging leaders to cultivate a feedback group comprised of other motivated professionals interested in gaining and giving input on performance and perception. While the recruitment of your 3 to 5 person group is not easy, a good support group is a source of frank feedback and idea exchange.

Define a group charter, ensure everyone is comfortable speaking openly about perceptions, and hold people accountable for input...as well as for actions. Politically motivated members and social loafers should be quickly benched in favor of others genuinely interested in giving and gaining.

2. Cultivate Your Social Intelligence and Skills.

Learning to assess and respond appropriately to the situation at hand is a core component of projecting your professional presence and building your brand. While this sounds a lot like playing politics…and it may be, it is at least being smart about how you participate. No one's asking you to nod your head blindly or, to compromise your morals. I am indicating that you should be smart enough and self-aware enough to adapt your style and approach to the situation. Make your point, but make it with grace and courtesy.

The inability to assess and respond appropriately in varying situations is a derailment factor for too many. We all know the person who never passes up an opportunity to stand-up and standout, often in an obnoxious and off-putting manner. You can be zealous in pursuit of your agenda without being a martyr.

3. Become a Network Connector.

Think in terms of organizational and industry ecosystems, not departments and functions. The better you are at building connections across the broader ecosystem, the more likely you are to gain access to unique information and insight into top talent. Cultivating an effective and growing network where you constantly strive to connect people (in contrast to just linking yourself into disparate groups) pays dividends for you and your network partners.

4. Learn to Lead both Vertically and Horizontally.

The most successful leaders understand that leadership isn't just a downward facing challenge. Effective leaders apply the tools in 1-3 above and cultivate their power and influence across organizations. They learn to involve others in pursuit of vexing organizational problems and improvements, and importantly, they learn how to make heroes out of others.

Managing up the ladder is one of the more important and in my experience, one of the most under-pursued critical professional activities. And no, sucking up to the boss, brown-nosing and generally serving as a brainless follower don't count!

Proper boss management requires you to invest time and energy to better understand and support or accommodate the boss's priorities, communication preferences and decision-making style. Remember, someone chooses you to be successful, and the boss usually gets a big vote.

The Bottom-Line for Now:

Self-development…it's hard work. It's also a full contact sport. Engage or expect to be left behind.

Chapter 7

Nine Ideas for Strengthening Your Self Esteem

One definition of self-esteem is: "confidence in one's own worth or abilities."
Another suggests: "Self-esteem is the experience of being competent to cope with
the basic challenges of life and being worthy of happiness."

While typically not a topic discussed over coffee, many leaders struggle with issues of low self-esteem. They question their ability to cope with the problems at hand, they often doubt they are worthy of the position of leadership they occupy, and they most definitely agonize quietly over much of their professional existence. Others manifest their low self-esteem with over-the-top aggressiveness and strong controlling behaviors.

Regardless of how the self-esteem issue is expressed, the sufferers struggle with a debilitating level of self-doubt. Unfounded criticism and minor setbacks easily derail the positive thought train. Instead of pursuing success, the leader with low self-esteem settles for survival.

9 Ideas to Help Strengthen Your Leadership Self-Esteem:

1. Recognize that you're not alone in your self-doubts. The greatest historical figures and leaders throughout history struggled with self-doubt, so you're in good company. Focus on the bigger purpose of your role.

2. Define your "bigger purpose." I crafted *The Leader's Charter* to remind me of my true role as a leader. A few moments reviewing and reflecting upon *The Charter* every morning, works wonders for my attitude and for providing a bigger reason for being.

The Leader's Charter:

Your primary role as a leader is to:

-Create an environment that facilitates high individual and team performance.

-Support innovation in process, programs and approaches.

-Encourage collaboration where necessary for objective achievement.

*-Promote the development of your associates in roles
that leverage their talents and interests
and that challenge them to new and greater accomplishments.*

With all of that "purpose" to focus on, it's hard to spend time wondering whether you are up to the job. The right actions and approaches towards others are spelled out in *The Charter*. And as you live your day(s) according to the concepts, you cannot help but produce small victories. These small victories are rocket-fuel for self-esteem.

3. Keep a list of the small victories to reinforce your growing self-esteem and good attitude. Remember to share the wealth by celebrating or praising the positive accomplishments of others. Your positive praise helps others build their own self-esteem.

4. Read something inspirational. My own doses of self-esteem fuel come from biographies of historical figures that battled overwhelming odds only to succeed. It's amazing what looking at a truly bad situation faced by someone else will do to put your own situation in proper perspective.

5. Only trust feedback from trusted sources. Not all feedback and not all feedback providers are created equal. The comment from an audience member recently regarding a concept that I "failed to develop" on one of my slides was interesting but frankly irrelevant. The talk had been a success, however, it clearly bugged this guy that I had not expanded upon the issue he felt so passionately about. I suggested he make it a self-study topic.

6. If you're stalled, take action. Actions and forward movement are important steps in building self-esteem. An internal preoccupation on your supposed negatives coupled with no action is truly self-reinforcing.

7. Focus your actions on your strengths. Just for a few moments, forget about the weaknesses that you believe are holding you back.

8. Don't overlook your physical appearance. Focus on getting in shape, getting a better haircut and/or improving your style of dress. Much of our self-esteem flows from how we feel about our looks and physical presence.

9. Selectively strengthen weaknesses. As the small victories pile up, and as you build upon your strengths and refocus your efforts around your priorities, selectively identify weaknesses to strengthen. Buy and read and apply the ideas in a self-help book, take a course or seek a mentor to guide your efforts and offer reinforcement.

The Bottom-Line for Now:

Your self-esteem is an intensely personal issue that impacts others and affects your ability to succeed. A strong sense of your own self-worth is important for building self-confidence, and self-confidence is an important ingredient for success as a leader. If you're struggling with a sense of low-self esteem, it's important to do something. Try the items on the list, add in others, and if you're still struggling, seek help. You deserve a strong feeling of self-esteem, and your colleagues deserve a leader with enough self-confidence to help them strive and succeed.

Section 2

Politics, Bosses and Other Realities of Organizational Life

D eath, taxes, bosses and organizational politics are four certainties of life. I'll leave the death and taxes stuff to others and focus here on the latter two issues. And as much as you would like to believe you're above playing politics or that you don't have to manage your boss, ignore these important issues and tasks at your own career peril. Fortunately, there are ways to do both while maintaining your dignity and your integrity. Read on for some guidance that may just alter (in the right way) the trajectory of your career.

Chapter 8

The Noble Pursuit of Power and Influence

Note from Art: no ethics or morals were harmed in the writing of this essay.

Power and influence are not dirty words. Both are components of every organization's environment and both must be carefully cultivated for you to succeed as a formal or informal leader.

Power and influence provide the motive power behind organizations and initiatives and the lubrication that keeps the parts and people from binding and grinding and self-destructing.

Nothing happens without the application of power and influence wielded by those that have carefully cultivated these qualities. And while the notion of someone actively pursuing power might seem reprehensible, dirty or immoral to some, I'm not sure why.

Frequently Overheard:

- *"I don't want to play the games."*

- *"I'm sick and tired of politics"*

- *And the always colorful and image evoking, "He must have pictures..."*

We've all heard these statements and perhaps nodded in agreement. Yet, the presence of humans in the working environment guarantees that there will be those that are more effective at connecting, engaging, motivating, and ultimately getting things done through others. And these aren't necessarily the smartest people or the hardest workers, but they are more than likely the smartest workers.

Intelligence is More than I.Q.

Those who cultivate power and influence work hard on managing themselves. They are emotionally intelligent. These power-pursuers are also innately aware of the impact they have on others, and they draw upon well-honed skills to manage external perceptions and to adapt to changing situations. They are socially intelligent.

Personal Branding & Building Respectful Relationships:

Those with power and influence have carefully thought through their own personal brands and value propositions, and they work hard reinforcing their brands through their actions and behaviors. Their focus is on getting work done through others and asserting their agenda, and to do that, they must forge respectful relationships, build strong social networks and create guiding coalitions, all the while remembering to provide support for others more often than they ask for support.

It's my informal observation that those who successfully cultivate organizational power and influence are masters at managing upwards. This is different than sucking up. It's understanding your manager's agenda and priorities and helping her succeed. It's leveraging your knowledge of those priorities to grow visibility, get involved with key projects and yes, even to curry support.

Backroom Dealers and Dirty Politicians Need Not Apply:

While the bad eggs in the corporate world grab the headlines and the cool orange prison garb that's been so fashionable with executives for the past decade, the gross majority of people in organizations do not resemble those characters. I've worked in and around companies with hundreds to hundreds of thousands of employees and while there have been some blog post worthy lousy leaders, they are the exception, not the rule.

From top executives to truly powerful individual contributors that serve as influencers on key strategic choices and projects, to those leading from the middle, there are great collectors and noble users of powers almost everywhere.

The abusers and the abusive exist and their tactics are reprehensible. I don't have an easy answer if you are victimized by one of those creatures, other than to indicate that if you improve your cultivation of power and influence, you will be better able to deal with or avoid the situation the next time.

Six Reasons Why Pursuing Power and Influence is a Good Career Move:

1. Your personal productivity will improve. Those with power and influence get more done. You can print this and put it on a bumper sticker!

2. Cultivating power and influence is honest, hard work that helps you hone your social skills. The pursuit of power and influence in an organization involves figuring out how to stand out from the crowd. This is generally best accomplished by some combination of darned hard work, great ideas, building good social networks and helping your boss succeed. Nothing wrong with those pursuits!

3. You build and strengthen your personal brand. The act of pursuing power is a personal branding activity. You have to decide what you stand for and you need to communicate and substantiate your value proposition through your actions. Of course, the pursuit of power and influence requires that you live up to your stated value proposition. People are generally not naïve and can smell hollow and inauthentic self-promotion a few miles away.

4. You cultivate critical growth skills. Gaining power and influence requires great people skills. Part of cultivating great people skills involves understanding how you are perceived by those around you, and this means that you must be alert and open to feedback and to making the effort to improve based on the feedback. This growing power and influence stuff is honest, hard work!

5. You create a multiplier effect. As you cultivate power, you have the ability to extend your good ideas and approaches across the organization. It's easy to talk about how you wish things would work. Those with power and influence are able to define how things truly work and extend their vision across teams and entire organizations.

6. You create demand for YOU. Your senior leaders want to see people with ambition, commitment and an interest in doing more. As long as your approach to growth doesn't involve stepping on the heads and hands of those that you are scrambling over, we really like aggressive people that are willing to help fight the good fight.

The Bottom-Line for Now:

The pursuit of power and influence is noble. Given the choice between an individual self-confident enough to cultivate power and one not interested in "playing the game," I know where I'm going every time. The real "game" is about winning by serving customers and stakeholders and legally beating the snot out of competitors. What's your strategy to grow your power?

Chapter 9

It's Time to Quit Blaming the Boss

The focus of this essay is to encourage a renewed sense of personal and professional accountability. Yep, I'm striking a blow against Boss-Blame...the world class sport that too many engage in as part of rationalizing why their own results might just be falling short of something resembling excellence.

D o not let the chucklehead (said with all due respect) you work for hold you back! Do not blame the management team for your inability to hit your targets, develop professionally or create a high performance team. The only one in charge of you is you!

I've long since concluded that *fixing* the bad bosses in the world is a losing proposition. All of us can work hard to become the type of boss that people are grateful for, and we can all work on developing new leaders on our teams who will develop into good bosses. However, in case you get stuck with a bad one for a period of time, here are some suggestions to help you cope.

How to Cope with a Bad Boss:

- **Change your behaviors.** I've observed many situations where the boss is openly criticized or even ridiculed. Fair warning: the water-cooler talk always makes it back to the boss, and the lack of respect simply pours fuel on the fire. A better approach than engaging in "boss bashing" with your coworkers, involves using judo on the situation. Try increasing your efforts to be respectful and helpful, and to portray a genuine sense of empathy for the burdens this individuals bears as a leader and as a person. Hey, no guarantees here, but you'll be the better person for trying, and it might buy you some latitude in the workplace.

- **Try partnering.** What is stopping you from working with your peers to focus your collective energies on eradicating the mostly controllable and predictable problems that bedevil so many teams? Nothing. Instead of blaming the boss, start working with your colleagues on finding productive solutions. And then implement them!

- **Don't expect coaching miracles.** You must develop your own sense of accountability. If you are not getting the support and coaching that you genuinely should receive, get over it and get on with it. And make certain that you go to extraordinary lengths to give to your colleagues what you are not receiving from your manager.

- **Not hearing much about your career path?** Here's my reminder, probably for the 50th time: you are in charge of your own career.

- **Don't get much feedback on your performance?** That's unfortunate, but it is not an excuse for you not recognizing that feedback is your most powerful performance tool and practicing it constantly with your own team members. And by the way, have you tried asking your boss for feedback? Many managers are so uncomfortable delivering feedback, they avoid it all costs. Show your boss you are concerned about improving and doing a better job, and she might just open up with you.

- **Does the boss work hard to protect turf and strengthen silo walls?** Don't fall into this shortsighted trap. Become a network broker across organizational boundaries. Learn and apply the art of lateral leadership and diplomacy.

The Bottom-Line for Now:

Just as it is common in life for people to hitch their sense of well-being and happiness to the actions and opinions of others, it is common for people to wallow in business misery because of the shortcomings of our leaders. It's time to unhitch that wagon and take responsibility for your own business happiness and health. Get started now.

Chapter 10

How to Handle a Feedback Attack from Your Boss

In spite of the best efforts of those of us that write and coach on leadership and feedback, there are still too many managers that wouldn't know how to construct an effective feedback discussion if their leadership lives depended on it.

The feedback tales that particularly bother me are the ones where the hard working employee is on the receiving end of a long laundry list of vague criticisms with an expiration date of several months ago.

These unfortunate feedback discussions are all about ego on the part of the giver and are perceived as a sneak attack by the receiver. The giver walks away feeling like he executed on his management tasks, and the receiver walks away feeling like he was nearly executed. People appropriately describe feeling angry, confused, frustrated and depressed after one or more feedback attacks.

While there's no doubt this is a tough situation for the receiver, there are a number of strategies that can take the sting out of the attack and help build or repair your relationship with your boss in the process. Fair warning! There are no guarantees in life or in attempting to rehabilitate a Feedback Attacker from a position of weakness. Nonetheless, you owe it to yourself, your boss and your career to try.

Eight Strategies for Recovering from a Feedback Attack:

1. Resist the Urge to Counterattack-It's normal for you to feel a range of emotions, including outrage and anger or extreme disappointment during a full-scale feedback attack. Earlier in my career, I would respond to a frontal assault with equal energy, and more than a couple of these discussions dissolved into something that I'm not proud of.

My hard-earned guidance is to recognize the situation for what it is, tell your mind and body to relax, and focus all of your energy on active listening. Your calm demeanor and attentiveness alone are enough to take a bit of wind out of the sails of some Feedback Attackers.

2. Recognize the Situation as a Process, Not an Event-The Feedback Attacker created an event, but you need to manage this as a multi-step process. You've already lost the skirmish and now you need to be able to walk away with good intelligence and all of your body parts and your job still intact.

3. Don't Confuse the Messenger's Style with the Message-This is my nice way of offering that sometimes there are nuggets of gold buried deep inside the heaping piles of feedback dung piling up around you. It is your job to put on the gloves and dig through the piles for anything of value.

4. Ask Questions, But Be Careful-Active listening involves you asking clarifying questions and ultimately, restating the answers in your own words and seeking confirmation. My caution on this one is that most Feedback Attackers are on pretty thin ice with their evidence. They don't have reasonable answers or specifics for your good and appropriate questions, and if you persist in asking questions, you will leave them no choice but to assert ego and position. It's easy to perceive and to mistake when a feedback receiver has shifted from the conversation at hand to building evidence for HR. It's not time to go there yet.

5. And More Active Listening-Don't leave the conversation without summarizing and restating the Attacker's concerns. Forget for a moment that in your mind it is unfounded. You must understand the concerns, no matter how vague they are.

6. Manage the Go-Forward Process-Most Feedback Attackers not only cannot substantiate their issues, they have no idea how to guide you on improving. It is essential that you seek agreement with your boss on a process for monitoring your progress. Indicate your interest in sitting down to discuss your progress on a regular basis going forward. And then do it! Along the way, you will show your interest in listening and improving, you will show your respect and you will be actively crafting your next review in real time with mutually developed evidence.

7. Work Harder at Managing Your Boss-The feedback process is often massacred by inexperienced and/or insecure managers that truly don't know what to do. You can respond with outrage and risk becoming a victim or, you can suck it up and work harder at understanding the issues, challenges and priorities of your boss, and then helping him or her with those priorities. Your active interest and visible support for your boss may eliminate the chances of future feedback attacks. In fact, you might just forge a good working relationship along the way.

8. Don't Fool Yourself By Being a Fool-If the boss is truly a Grade-A jerk and your attempts at building a bridge are met with more dynamite, you are not going to win. You can HOPE (a bad strategy) that he/she will go somewhere else, but you've got to face reality. You may need to vote yourself off the island.

The Bottom-Line for Now:

Feedback Attackers are petty tyrants and inexperienced leaders seeking to establish authority through control. While fighting back might feel right in the moment, it's never the right thing to do. Don't ignore the attack...it is very real and that attitude from your boss is a warning sign.

Instead, politely and professionally grab control of the process and genuinely work to improve and to communicate. You might just be helping someone grow up as a leader while you are protecting and enhancing your job.

Chapter 11

How to Cope with Organizational Alchemists

The modern-day practice of alchemy is only metaphorically about the search for a method to turn lead into gold. Instead of the medieval pursuit by alchemists of a magical chemical conversion process to change one element into another, modern practitioners are focused on the magical and easy transformation of people and organizations from one level of performance to another. Modern day, organizational alchemists are looking for great results but aren't interested in participating in the hard work required to produce these results.

W hile the vocation of Alchemist is long dead, you see modern practitioners at work every day.

Examples of Modern Organizational Alchemists:

- Executives who talk endlessly about the need for change, yet, never put any effort into the hard work of enabling change.

- Executives who turn their quarterly prognostications into actual numbers, offering up this weak proof that their Alchemist's Ways work. Jim Goodnight, CEO of the wildly successful and privately-held (by him)

SAS Institute, offered in a fascinating interview on Sixty Minutes a number of years ago: *"There's only one way that I know of to accurately hit the quarterly numbers, and that is to cook the books."* Dr. Deming shared a similar perspective.

- Leaders who use leadership training programs as easy substitutes for the hard work of developing others on their teams.

- Firms and executives who delegate the identification of value creating and differentiating strategies to consultants, and ignore the hard-won experience and knowledge of their own employees.

- Management teams that talk about being market-driven and customer-focused, without actually translating those nice words into anything meaningful in terms of processes and performance standards.

- Leaders who expect employees to be creative on command.

- Managers and leaders who refuse to say "No," and consistently flood their employees with a dizzying and disorienting array of projects. Everything is a priority, but nothing gets done.

My best advice for coping with these characters is to invoke the Anti-Alchemist's philosophy. *"If it's worth doing, it's worth working hard for."* (I believe most of us probably heard this repeatedly from our parents at an early age.) This goes for creating hit products, improving sales performance, developing people, improving customer service, creating high performance teams and every other single activity worth doing and worth improving in your organization. There are no shortcuts.

A Dozen Questions Guaranteed to Make Alchemist's of all Sizes, Levels and Shapes Vaporize (or at least squirm):

1. How do you envision this helping us?

2. Why is this a good strategic direction?

3. What do you mean by customer-focused?

4. What we will look like and act like as a firm when we're customer focused?

5. What do you mean by market-driven?

6. If we're going to invest our hard earned money in this training program, what are we going to do differently after the program to apply the lessons learned?

7. How are you and the other executives going to help us knock down some of the impediments to progress that we all see and know but don't talk about?

8. What does that feedback mean? Specifically, what behavior do you want me to change?

9. How many customers did we talk to in the making of this strategy?

10. Why do you trust outside advisors more than the people that work here?

11. Which project do you want us to drop to take on your new top priority?

12. What's your part in our team's success?

The Bottom-Line for Now:

If you're in a leadership role, ask and answer the above questions yourself before opening your mouth and exposing your Alchemist's ways to your team members. If you work for an Alchemist, recognize that the above questions won't magically transform this person. Use the questions carefully, teach the questions to your team members and politely, firmly and consistently seek answers.

Chapter 12

Learn to Make Quick Connections

In a typical, fast moving day, there are dozens of small opportunities for leaders to make or strengthen connections with team members and peers. Effective leaders strive to leverage these fleeting moments as golden opportunities to show respect, strengthen connections and even support coalition building. The trick is to execute a deliberate "connection" strategy throughout your day.

5 Ideas for Quickly Connecting On-the-Run:

1. The Eyes Have It-In a large corporate environment where you encounter hundreds or more people per day, constantly connect with your eyes and your smile. I don't care if you are walking from your car to your office or heading towards the company cafeteria for lunch, you've got a chance to engage a great number of people in a hurry...don't waste it. Being recognized...even if it's just a smile, direct eye contact and a friendly nod, serves up a spark of energy for both receiver and giver.

2. Provide Public Praise Where Appropriate-As you encounter teams or project groups in the course of your day, never pass up an opportunity to offer supporting (and specific) praise. Do the same for individuals, however, be sensitive to social factors that might create embarrassment for the recipient. Absolutely deliver well-deserved praise in one-on-one situations.

3. Show Interest by Asking Questions-If you're in charge, you're supposed to know what's going on, so don't be shy about asking questions. A good tactic is to check-in on status and to ask whether there's anything you can do to support the effort. Your inquiry PLUS your offer shows concern and commitment...much better than an openly invasive grilling. Of course, if someone has something for you to do, make certain and take care of it as quickly as possible.

4. Extend Invitations on the Go-*"Jen, I would love to catch up on the Alpha project you are spearheading. Drop me a note and I will find a spot in my calendar as soon as you are ready."* Again, you're showing interest and commitment, and your offer to adjust your calendar displays importance and respect.

5. Broker Introductions-Good leaders recognize the importance of helping others make connections. Go out of your way to identify and involve other groups and individuals in the organization that might be interested in knowing what's going on with particular projects and programs. If you're not certain whom to involve, reach out to a peer or executive and extend an invitation.

The Bottom-Line for Now:

A chance encounter is a horrible thing to waste. Too many managers roll through their days on a mission chasing the urgent and the urgent-unimportant, without investing any time cultivating relationships. Develop the good habit of leveraging casual and fast encounters to pay respect, show interest and offer help, and you'll single-handedly raise the office energy level.

Chapter 13

How to Appropriately Respond to Positive Praise

It's easy to start believing the praise you hear in the hallways about your leadership approach. Easy and dangerous.

I've always been leery of the unfounded and saccharine-sweet praise that is bestowed upon leaders. While you may call me cynical, I prefer to think of myself as pragmatic.

Praise Goeth Before the Fall:

Your employees may genuinely like and respect you, however, the best measure of your performance is not their praise for you, but rather, it's their performance on your team.

We like to hear nice things about ourselves, and employees are quick to figure out that you respond positively to their praise. If there were an Office Olympics, Boss-Praise would be a major medal category, right after Boss-Bashing. If there's even the remotest evidence that you respond favorably to subtle or blatant sucking up, I guarantee that you'll be buried under an avalanche of false praise. You need to maintain objectivity at all times. A hunger for praise will compromise that objectivity.

49

You earn your leadership credibility every single day. Start believing your own press clippings and you're likely to back off of your own performance accelerator. Take the praise too seriously, and you're likely to back off the accelerator, pop the performance gear into neutral and start coasting. Downhill.

As for the boss offering up praise for your work, we really love to hear it. However, knowing that most managers struggle to deliver the constructive kind of feedback, the positive praise may very well be a misguided attempt to manage you by feeding your ego. It's easier to make you feel good than it is to highlight specific instances where YOU need to improve.

Five Ideas for Coping with Positive Praise:

Yeah, I know. The words are nice to hear. They help you define your own sense of self-worth. We all want to be appreciated. There are some good habits in coping with positive praise, including:

1. Always receive praise graciously. In spite of my apparent cynicism on this topic, it is possible that the praise you are receiving is genuine and heartfelt.

2. Look for the nuggets that explain what you did that merited the praise. You want to find the behaviors that are appreciated and reinforce them in your daily activities.

3. Teach people through your response to praise. In an environment where it appears people are seeking favor through praise, politely counter with statements like, "Thank you. Now, what is it I can do better to help this team succeed?" After a few rounds of questions, people will begin to understand that you don't respond to disingenuous praise, and importantly, they will see that you are truly focused on improving your daily performance. Your attitude and your positive behaviors will prove infectious in the workplace!

4. Put a positive-praising boss at ease by seeking out the constructive feedback. Once you clearly communicate that you genuinely like the constructive input, the boss's fear of feedback may melt.

5. Teach your team how to dispense proper positive praise. Liberally dispense positive praise of your own. Ensure that it is behavioral and tied to the business. Your team members will quickly catch on to the pattern.

The Bottom-Line for Now:

Always remember that you're not working for praise, you're working for results. Measure your success by how well your team members succeed and grow as professionals. Experienced leaders know that the highest form of praise that they can receive is watching those that they've supported go on to successful roles and careers. And every once in awhile, someone will look back and say, "Thank you." Now that's praise that you can take to heart.

Chapter 14

Nine Great Habits in Boss Management

Woe to the person that fails to properly manage his or her boss. And don't confuse the concept of managing the boss with anything that resembles shameless sucking-up or its close cousin, brown-nosing.

While some bosses are more challenging than others, you are well served to give it your best shot to understand as much about your boss's working style, priorities, expectations and aspirations as possible.

Learning to work with and yes, manage the person that you work for is a critical issue in ensuring your short-term success and long-term professional sanity. Those interested in digging into some of the formative work on "boss management" are encouraged to check out the work of John Kotter and John Gabarro, including their formative article, *"Managing the Boss,"* published originally in Harvard Business Review. For now, here's a quick checklist to help remind you of some best practices that you can apply immediately:

Nine Great Habits in Boss Management:

1. Keep the boss appropriately informed. You should gauge his/her need for information volume and frequency and adapt to it. Also, remember that some bosses are "readers" and some are "listeners." Don't overwhelm a "listener" with reports and don't expect verbal updates to cut it with "readers."

2. Prove your credibility daily. Honesty is the only policy. Never give a boss a reason to doubt your word.

3. Your boss's priorities are your priorities. Learn them, live them, work them.

4. Know the boss's pet programs. See also the priority note. Find ways to support and extend those programs across the organization.

5. Learn your boss's aspirations. Help a great boss achieve his/her aspirations and you'll benefit in the process. Help a lousy boss do the same and you've solved a problem.

6. Know your boss's organizational heroes. Seek opportunities to help bring them and you together.

7. Outside interests? Make them yours if you can be genuine. While it might be hard for you to fake interest in WWF Wrestling or Tractor Pulling or whatever slightly off-the-beaten path interest your boss has, you are well served to show interest if he does. Many rankle at this as the purest form of sucking up. If the interest is forced, I agree. However, having grown up in a household where it was common for our family to take ski vacations and ride motorcycles with my Dad's boss and coworkers, I know that the interest can be genuine. Use your judgment here, and if interests collide and if there's not awkwardness in sharing a hobby, then go for it. Just don't force it.

8. Resist the urge to publicly disagree with your boss. Speak up respectfully in private if you have to, but don't light a boss-bridge on fire in a public setting. The quick combustion might just consume you.

9. Negative Boss Talk. It's easy to fall into this trap. Never, ever, ever engage in negative boss talk. Run, don't walk, in the other direction.

The Bottom-Line for Now:

There's nothing manipulative or even disingenuous about working to manage your boss. This is simply another opportunity to develop your skills at engaging with others, collaborating with the person that for a moment in time decides whether you are successful or not, and serving as a follower. If the roles were reversed, I suspect that you would appreciate the active efforts of your employees to support, help and get to know you.

Chapter 15

If the Boss Asks You the Time, Don't Tell Her How to Build a Watch

Just about everyone knows someone that never read the memo on how to get to the point in conversations. I warmly reference these people as Watchmakers. Instead of giving you the time of day when you ask for it, they tell you in painful detail how to build the watch.

W hile command of detail is impressive, the need to share it with everyone that you come in contact with can be debilitating to your career. Bosses avoid opening even casual conversations, groups are hesitant to draw watchmakers into discussions and co-workers have been known to begin thinking of creative ways to extract themselves from your conversations, even as you are approaching.

Any Watchmakers in Your Life (or, Are You One)?

I come from a long family of digressers on one side of my family, and conversations with these wonderful people are truly amazing adventures. You start out heading in one direction and thirty minutes later you realize you've been around the world on a verbal odyssey with no logical beginning or ending.

It's a challenge and a great deal of fun to try and nicely manage the conversation towards your original inquiry. We tolerate this at home fairly well, however, at work, it's just annoying.

Unfortunately, most Watchmakers don't recognize their communication approach and its limitations, and they are dependent upon some courageous colleague or a boss comfortable in delivering feedback for this eye-opening and hopefully, mouth-closing coaching. Perhaps you're a Watchmaker, and no one has worked up the courage to confront you with this news. Or perhaps, you've never given them enough time and oxygen to pass the message along!

Three Tips to Learn to Tell the Time...Not How to Build the Watch:

Whether you are the Watchmaker in question or you manage one of these individuals, here are some tips for helping them do a better job staying on-point:

1. Brevity is power when it comes to getting your point across. Help Watchmakers understand the importance of brevity in formal settings... especially with senior managers or customers. Ensure that you provide tangible examples that you've observed and tie this good feedback to business issues, personal and group effectiveness and performance.

2. Encourage pre-thinking of key message points for planned, formal settings. I use a technique that I learned from a P.R. pro called message mapping. This can be done in a matter of minutes...and I use it constantly. Describe your core point in the center of the map...allow four branches for supporting points...and then link each supporting point with one or two branches for additional detail. The key to the message map is then to use it to make points and answer questions. While it takes some practice to perfect, this technique can truly help increase the relevance and impact of your brief points.

3. Teach Watchmakers to learn to flip the switch. Learning to recognize impending communication situations and trigger the response of "OK, I need to make my key point and nothing more," is a difficult but necessary habit to form. Perhaps it's a bit of classical conditioning, but the best communicators run through this pre-event processing to determine what they will say and how they will conduct themselves. I'm convinced that this is something that can be learned and reinforced with help from an observant manager, mentor or friend.

The Bottom-Line for Now:

While it's difficult to change your core communication style, it is important to recognize the need in many circumstances for clarity and brevity. A college professor of mine always included the following statement on the top of his exams: "Brevity displays knowledge of the subject matter." Those words have echoed in my mind for the past two decades.

Regale your family with stories and digress to your heart's content around the kitchen table. But when it comes to work, get on-point, make and reinforce your point and then be quiet! Get good at this and you'll actually create more opportunities to contribute!

Chapter 16
The Importance of Cultivating Influence

How much influence do you have as a leader in your organization?

While it's not something that probably crosses your mind on a daily basis, your relative influence in your organization is one reasonable proxy for your effectiveness as a leader.

Much like trust, the precious commodity of influence is earned over time based on a great number of exposures. True influence isn't bestowed by a title. It's born of hard work. Your personal bank account of influence is developed early in a career by working in the trenches, doing your part to master your craft, doing what you say you'll do and treating others with respect. Add in a dash of helping others…newcomers and those that can use a boost, and suddenly a positive view on you begins to emerge.

She's someone we respect.

He's someone who walks the talk.

Respect Begets Trust and Trust is the Foundation of Influence.

Leaders have the added challenge of growing influence on a larger playing field, and this involves dealing with the Double P... Power & Politics. Ignore these at your own peril. Learn to understand where power lies and cultivate your skills in legitimately pursuing power, and you will grow your influence. Be aware of politics, and instead of denying it, use *ethical finesse* in coping with and managing it. Eyes wide open, please.

3 Keys to Cultivating Power and Growing Influence:

Power is usually waiting for someone to pick it up and run with it.

1. Find problems.

2. Involve others and start fixing the problems.

3. Create heroes.

Ten Questions to Help Assess Your Level of Influence:

1. Are you often selected to participate (or better yet, lead) high visibility projects?

2. Are your former team members well established in positions of authority around the organization?

3. Is your function or team a destination of choice for high quality people from across your business?

4. Are you asked to mentor others, or, do you serve as an informal mentor for people from around the organization?

5. Are you visible to senior managers and executives as someone who makes things happen?

6. Do other managers ask about and recruit the talent on your team?

7. Are you known as a leader who helps people push through job level and compensation limits?

8. Are you known for helping people create careers?

9. Are you well networked (beyond the superficial level) in your organization, from top to bottom?

10. Can you get senior-level face time when you ask for it?

The Bottom-Line for Now:

If you can answer a good number of the ten questions above in the affirmative, you are on your way to cultivating ethical influence. If the answers are genuinely, "no," it's time for some leadership soul searching. Find some people you trust and ask for input. You might want to be sitting down when they hit you with their thoughts and perceptions.

Those with influence define the rules, select the players and enjoy the outcomes. Perhaps it's time to begin deliberately and ethically working on cultivating your workplace influence.

Section 3

The Leader and Decisions

Decision-making is daily exercise for the leader's mind. Ultimately, you are as effective and as successful as the decisions you make and implement. You will face big calls, including choosing strategic directions, selecting projects and products to invest in, and choosing between really capable people to fill key positions. The big decisions tend to be exercises in coping with ambiguity and managing overwhelming volumes of information. However, in-between every couple of major calls, you face literally thousands of slightly less significant, but still important decisions. People will look to you for direction on priority calls and they will seek your input or blessing on their own big decisions. Frankly, your days will be so filled with making or helping make decisions, that by the time you get home and your significant other asks, "what should we have for dinner?" your mind may feel like it will literally melt down and run out your ears if you have to process anything that complicated.

As a leader, you have two principal issues to deal with when it comes to making decisions. You've got to cultivate your own skills and style in the art and science of decision-making, and you've got to learn how to teach others to do the same for themselves. Remember, leaders teach. Having said that, don't sign on for any teaching assignments in this arena until you've spent some quality time of your own studying the processes and pitfalls of individual and team decision-making. Your first assignment is to read this section from end-to-end and put the concepts into practice in your everyday work life. After you've spent some quality time working on cultivating your own decision-making style and strengthening your effectiveness, you can begin the important process of helping others do the same.

Chapter 17

The Triple Threat to Good Decisions: Data, Time and Emotion

There are few situations more challenging to teams than dealing with a tough, emotionally charged issue and decision-choice while facing significant time pressures and seemingly contradictory data.

If the situation described above sounds uncommon or unrealistic, consider that many firms and management teams make critical priority calls and strategic choices under just such circumstances. The decision to launch the Challenger was a prime example, with all three factors: emotion, time pressure and contradictory data, playing a huge role in this tragic call. Countless corporate strategic misfires owe their outcome to this triple-threat of data, time and emotion.

While many situations don't involve life-safety issues, this triple-threat is something that every manager should be critically sensitive to in their group and strategic decision-making.

Data, Bloody Data:

Let's start here first. All of us would like to believe that we are making data-driven, fact-based calls on key issues. Unfortunately, the data quality facts don't back that opinion.

Our firms have invested small fortunes in powerful data warehousing, enterprise management and analytic software programs, yet report after report substantiates that the data in our systems is crap. It's poor quality, obsolete and just plain wrong. And beyond the fatal data quality issues, we struggle with too much information and the very real and challenging issue of how to interpret the data.

How We Play Data Roulette:

- Looking for the data that confirms our opinion and then seizing upon this confirming evidence at the expense of a potentially contradictory error.

- Sampling on the dependent variable instead of the independent variable. This common logic error has people looking at the wrong issue and improperly attributing cause and effect.

- Ignoring the data. Given the volume of data typically just a click away, it's easy for individuals and groups to quickly become confused or overwhelmed. Another outcome of too much data is analysis paralysis.

Time after Time:

Most timelines for business initiatives are contrived, yet many managers and groups allow artificial deadlines to impact the quality of their decisions. Certainly, we all know that time is money and that windows of opportunity can close, and yet, I wouldn't let either of those clichés drive me to make a poor quality decision. I'll accept that speed of decision-making is important, but only if it is counter-balanced with quality.

Watch Out When Emotions Rule the Day:

My favorite, nausea inducing line of all is, "You've got to take off your (insert your functional hat) and put on your business hat." That invitation to suspend logic, slice your IQ and commonsense in half and make a poor call is often a ploy to both manipulate and to quickly resolve an emotion-laden issue by imploring someone to suspend judgment.

We don't make good decisions under emotional stress, and that goes for relationships and major life events as well as business situations. We fear change and will almost always opt for the decision that most resembles the status quo. We pursue consensus because we fear conflict. We make gut calls based on our emotions when faced with ambiguous data. We grab hold of data that confirms our perspectives and then we shut out potentially contradictory data. Overall, we are brilliant at finding ways to make lousy decisions, and when emotions enter the picture, we're often at our decision-making worst.

7 Suggestions to Lock Out the Triple Headed Monster of Poor Decision-Making:

As the leader, you are on the hook for teaching your team to make good decisions. Your firm depends upon it and your career depends upon it.

1. Strive for Crystal Clarity on the Issue! Frame the issue and carefully conduct a process- check to ensure that you are all looking at the same core issue and decision.

2. Hit the Brakes! If time-pressure takes over, it's your job to hit the brakes! I'm not certain of attribution, but the phrase: "slow down and think carefully before you do something stupid" jumps to mind here.

3. Hit the Brakes, Part 2! Too many managers are fearful of raising their hands and saying, "hold it." As a leader, foster a culture where people don't get kneecapped for pulling the chain to stop the production line, and as a professional, develop a spine.

4. Just the Facts! Spend time assessing what you know, and very importantly, defining what you still need to know to make a decision. The "what do we need to know?" part is often skipped.

5. Turn Data Into Information and Knowledge. Monitor data integrity and quality, and work with your group to carefully wrap it in meaning. This step is the source of many of the errors described above, so note your assumptions, watch out for framing and confirming evidence errors. Consider involving objective 3rd parties to help look at and interpret the data and data needs.

6. Recall Drucker's Saying: "Every Decision is a Risk-Taking Judgment." Teach your team to think through and prioritize on risks. Use face-to-face and anonymous input to ensure that risks are identified without the bias of social interaction.

7. Vent the Emotions and Then Move On. Edward De Bono's *Six Thinking Hats* approach to discussion and decision-making helps teams vent emotions in a constructive manner. Use his process, or, at least create an opportunity for everyone to vent and then challenge them to focus on facts, risks, opportunities and ideas. (The *Six Thinking Hats* process has the potential to significantly improve discussion and decision quality. Consider identifying an experienced facilitator to help you with this process.)

The Bottom-Line for Now:

Time pressures, emotional factors and data issues are at the root of many poor life and business decisions. High performance teams and effective leaders recognize these factors, talk openly about them when they start to encroach, and work hard at locking them back in their cage when quality of judgment is in danger. It's time to slay this triple-threat to effective decision-making in your environment.

Chapter 18

Developing Decision-Making Strength by Keeping a Decision-Journal

Your decisions define you as a leader and a manager, yet we spend very little time in our busy lives finding ways to improve our abilities in this area. A great place to start is by keeping a Decision Journal.

> *"Every decision is a risk-taking judgment."* –Peter Drucker

"Making decisions is the most important job of any executive. It's also the toughest and the riskiest." –Hammond, Keeney and Raifa in HBR, The Hidden Traps in Decision Making.

How many decisions do you make in a typical week? If you're like most managers, the answer is: "a bunch."

Many of our decisions are fairly straightforward. We have policies, procedures and precedent, and the decisions are effectively programmed. No sweat, limited risk and in fact, it's easy to train others to make these decisions. It's when we move outside of the programmed decisions that things get interesting.

The Sticky Decisions that Define Our Careers:

Consider the issue of choosing between multiple candidates for a job or, choosing which projects to invest in and which to place on the shelf. Compared to the programmed decisions, the way forward for these key decisions is clouded by all sorts of factors: political and business risks, fuzzy information, evaluation errors, biases, opinions, agendas and good old-fashioned ambiguity.

To make matters worse, the effectiveness of the decision is often not visible for some time and even that may prove hard to measure based on the effectiveness of the actions taken to implement the decision.

You Must Develop as an Effective Decision Maker to Climb the Ladder:

As you climb the ladder, the decisions become more ambiguous, more complex and a whole heck of a lot riskier. Of course, you won't reach the next rung on the ladder unless those above you develop confidence in your ability to navigate those issues.

Given the import of decision-making on your career, your firm and even your life, it's important to build decision-making muscle by scrutinizing your processes, your practices and your outcomes. A great place to start is to follow in the footsteps of da Vinci, Franklin, Jefferson and Drucker (just to name a few) and start a Decision Journal.

Improve Your Decision Making Muscle by Creating a Decision Journal:

First, I'll tackle the "this is corny" issue. Get over it. Our memories are ridiculously imperfect (a decision making trap!) and it's critical to capture some key points at the time you make the decision, to be able to effectively scrutinize the effectiveness of the decision some time in the future. Oh, and the list of Hall of Fame Decision Journal Keepers above isn't too shabby.

Note: this is useful for teams as well, and in project management circles, the use of a decision-log is a good practice.

At Least 12 Items to Capture in Your Decision Journal:

1. Decisions that are more strategic in nature, including hiring, promotions, project choices, investments, competitive moves and anything beyond the programmed level described above.

2. A clear statement of the issue and circumstances surrounding the issue. Specifically, how was the issue framed at the time of the decision?

3. The perceived risks you assessed as part of the decision making process.

4. The information you referenced to support the process.

5. The individuals (and your relationship to them) you called upon for input.

6. The individuals involved in directly making the decision and their opinions.

7. Emotional factors and other pressures (e.g. time) swirling around the issue.

8. The decision choices and how you evaluated them, including your assumptions.

9. A description of the planned process for moving from decision to implementation.

10. The expected outcome of the decision. What will determine success or failure?

11. How you will monitor the results of the decision?

12. When you expect to reasonably be able to assess the outcome?

And don't forget to leave a big space for results.

The Bottom-Line for Now:

This might seem like hard work. Well, it is, and there's some time involved in both recording the information above and importantly, looping back to describe outcomes and assess what you did right or wrong. However, if making good decisions is as important as I described it above (and it is!), how can you afford to not take the time?

How you record or capture is less important than the act of doing it, as long as the information is organized and accessible. We live in a world filled with productivity apps. From my favorite…a Moleskin notebook to various digital tools, there's little excuse other than laziness for not doing this.

Chapter 19
Mind the Decision Traps

First, the bad news. Most decision traps are invisible.

In my essay on developing a Decision-Journal, I emphasized the importance of incorporating this tool as a part of your program to improve your decision-making effectiveness. The Journal is used to log key decisions, assumptions and information about the decision-process and players for reference at a later date.

Without this type of a data trail, you are relying on your ability to recall the circumstances surrounding the decision. Unfortunately, psychologists have shown consistently that our perception of our ability to recall grossly exceeds the reality. Interestingly, this gap between our perception and our true ability is one of the classic cognitive biases or decision traps, and serves as an excellent lead-in to our exploration of these traps.

While clearly out of my competence zone on the neuroscience of brain function, a good number of researchers and scientists summarize our decision-making process as one of Pattern Matching coupled with Emotional Tagging. We process situations based on prior experience looking for signs of patterns, and once recognized, we attach stored emotional tags to those situations. Much of this happens in the background, with neurons firing in many areas of our brains simultaneously. Our first recognition of the output is often what we describe as our "gut" feeling about a situation.

The system works well for most familiar situations, however, it is not without its imperfections. In particular, as we are exposed to new situations that "don't compute," our response and decisions are potentially based on invalid patterns.

The flaws in the machine here tend to deal with various cognitive biases that lead us into decision-making traps with alarming regularity. The results can be inconvenient to catastrophic for our teams, our organizations and ourselves.

When the Pattern Didn't Match:

In one of my favorite articles on this topic, "Why Good Leaders Make Bad Decisions," at HBR, the authors describe how Matthew Broderick (the general…not the actor who played the character Ferris Bueller and then later married the actress, Sarah Jessica Parker), the head of the Homeland Security Operations Center during Hurricane Katrina, fell victim to a pattern-matching error.

Broderick, who had served in Vietnam, learned that early reports of disasters were often very wrong, and he developed a process of waiting for the "ground truth" to validate or invalidate the initial information. This served him well on the battlefield, and it also worked fine later at Homeland Security during other Hurricane situations. Of course, all of those other hurricanes took place around cities above sea level…a very different situation from New Orleans.

Through a series of conflicting reports, including a CNN report of people allegedly partying on Bourbon Street, Broderick closed the day by indicating in a situation report that the levees had not been breached, although this would require re-checking the next day. And then he went home.

Broderick was a victim of his own pattern-matching approach, and his experience in seeking and relying on the ground truth let him down (and many others) in a situation that was slightly different from his store of experiences.

More Bad News-There is No Cure:

The painful reality: there are a great number of ways our memories, our biases, and our emotional filters can lead us astray as we pursue the process of making decisions. Add in group dynamics and all of the other social factors in team settings, and the odds of getting it wrong go up tremendously.

Unfortunately, there are no simple cures for avoiding decision-making traps and cognitive biases. The best offense in this case is a strong defense, built on awareness of the traps and hypersensitivity to how situations are framed and decisions developed. Of course, for those offensive minded players and coaches, once your strong defense is in place, building processes and strengthening the culture to avoid the traps is eminently appropriate.

Vigilance is Key and Forewarned is Forearmed:

In subsequent essays, we explore some of the more vexing decision traps and cognitive biases in detail. Here's a quick list of some common traps.

- **Escalation of Commitment/Sunk Cost Trap**: the irrational pursuit of a failed approach. *Once you know the signs, you'll recognize this trap at work in the workplace…and as something that a quick read of the headlines will tell you, many firms fall victim to.*

- **Over-Confidence Bias and other Estimating and Forecasting Errors:** *your leadership style and the culture in your organization contribute to costly estimating and forecasting issues of all sorts. And mix a group in the equation, and watch out for a really dangerous level of over-confidence to emerge.*

- **Status Quo Trap:** *given our druthers, we will typically opt for the decision that best defends the status quo. While there are places and cases for this, the historical record of business is littered with organizations that never emerged from this trap.*

- **Groupthink:** *everyone thinks of Kennedy and the Bay of Pigs fiasco, but rest assured, you and your team members are quite susceptible to the suspension of reality and suppression of contradictory opinions that characterize this dangerous trap.*

- **Framing errors:** *how an issue is framed… and whether it is framed in terms of gains or losses will most definitely impact the choices developed and the final decision.*

- **Anchoring Traps:** *our own biases, the first information we hear, casual comments from colleagues are all contributors to our propensity to grab hold of early information and then view all other subsequent data through that filter.*

- **Confirming Evidence Bias:** *imagine our excitement when we find data to support our perspective. How objective are we about contradictory data? Turns out…not so much.*

The Bottom-Line for Now:

Like it or not, we don't make decisions precisely the way the textbooks describe the process. The perfect view of the decision-making process involves: defining the problem and the criteria for evaluating the problem, gathering and assessing the data, identifying options and then selecting the best option based on the criteria established at the beginning of the process. While this is more right than wrong, and we might work through those phases, there's often nothing rational about how we navigate each one. And we most definitely don't always make the "rational choices" that economists would have us believe are the only appropriate outcomes.

This is a big topic…with HUGE leadership and management implications. The first step is awareness of the issues. Remember, forewarned is forearmed. Here's to better decisions!

Chapter 20
Better Framing for More Effective
Decision-Making

"How we frame a problem often shapes the solution at which we arrive."
-Professor Michael Roberto

We tend to view the world as individuals and organizations through frames, nicely described by Professor Michael Roberto as: *"mental models that we use to simplify our understanding of the complex world around us, to help us make sense of it. They involve our assumptions, often taken for granted about how things work."*

A Few Really Big Examples:

Up until the moment of the terrorist attacks on that awful September day in 2001, the primary focus for defense planning purposes of the U.S. Government was the threat posed by other nation-states. This thinking was a carry over from the Cold War days, which had ended more than a decade earlier.

Analysis of General Motors documentation from the early 1970's indicated the following:

- The U.S. market is too isolated to be impacted by foreign automobile manufacturers.

- Fuel will be plentiful and inexpensive for years to come.

- Americans don't care about quality. They want style and will upgrade every 18 months to 2 years.

- We must promote our managers from within to secure our culture.

- We're in the business of making money, not cars.

And one of my famous quotes from GM: *"We don't need to make better cars, we need better customers."*

As the world changed, GM's rigid views made it nearly impossible for management to properly interpret, much less respond to, changing conditions.

And:

Starbucks has consistently thought of itself as, *The Third Place*, right after home and work. *Third Place* thinking guided the development of the in-store experience where people felt welcomed and were encouraged to linger and relax. As the chain lost focus on this frame and flooded the stores with new programs and products at a rapid clip, the stores began to lose this atmosphere and customers voted with their wallets and their feet.

A return to the original *Third Place* formula was one part of the turnaround that Howard Schultz and team engineered upon Howard's return to the CEO role a few years ago.

What the Studies Show:

Researchers have shown that our frames drive our decisions. A situation framed as a negative (a loss, a dire problem or a big risk) tends to evoke riskier responses than a situation framed as a positive.

A number of famous studies depict business or medical situations with identical outcomes (i.e. identical expected $ values or human outcomes) presented as both a negative and a positive. Our responses reinforce the perspective that we'll take more chances when faced with a negative frame and we'll act more conservatively when faced with a positive frame.

Leaders & Teams-Your Frames Drive Decisions:

We're constantly constructing and acting upon the frames that define our view to the world, and of course, we're making decisions based on these frames. And while framing is essential in our pursuit to understand and cope in the world, it also opens us up a host of potential decision-making pitfalls.

As a leader, your view to the world (your frame) has a powerful influence on your team members. To the extent they understand your frame, it becomes their frame, and they make decisions and priority calls accordingly. It works great if your frame is fairly neutral or, if your view is particularly accurate. However, paint a picture of an issue or situation as particularly positive or negative, or force your own potentially biased assumptions on a frame, and you create a cascading set of decision-making nightmares.

Groups form frames based on the individual views of the members and their ability to roll those views and assumptions into some form of "common view." Of course, personal biases, politics, egos, power and other socialization issues, along with diversity of experience, access to data and many others all impact and potentially skew our frames.

What's a Leader or Team to Do?

1. Awareness and Vigilance: there are no cures for Decision-Making traps, but as the saying goes, forewarned is forearmed. Be conscious of how you, your colleagues and your groups are framing issues and be aware of how these frames may skew idea generation and decisions.

2. Create Multiple Frames for Vexing Problems: for example, a firm's leaders viewing social networking as a waste of time might cultivate a highly restrictive policy, and minimize or eliminate any experimentation with these tools. It invites a "How can we restrict?" response.

An alternative frame of: "this is a big trend, how can we safely use social networking tools to better engage with our customers?" will invoke a completely different set of responses.

3. Frame Issues as Neutral: instead of introducing the biases observed in the studies towards risk-taking or risk-avoiding behavior based on whether a situation is framed as a negative or a positive, be careful to frame your situation as neutral. For example, "our competitor introduced a product at a brand new price and feature point," versus a "We're going to get hammered this quarter by our competitor's new product." The neutral wording will facilitate exploration of both opportunities (a rising tide and new market segment…along with a heavy learning curve for competitors), while the negative wording may invoke a crisis mentality and response.

4. Boss Hold Back: your framing of a situation will guide everyone else. If you are looking for creative ideas, don't communicate your frame in advance.

5. Always Seek to Understand How Others are Framing an Issue: ask questions, clarify assumptions and if your co-workers or team members are falling into some of the framing traps described above, suggest neutral approaches, multiple frames and draw in outside perspectives.

The Bottom-Line for Now:

The world is tough enough without fighting our own human tendencies to interject noise into the environment. You've been forewarned, and now you are forearmed. Frame your situations like a management craftsperson. Measure twice, cut once.

Chapter 21
Beware Estimating and Forecasting Traps

Poor management and leadership practices make a tough job tougher by introducing pressures and biases that directly impact estimating and forecasting activities.

If these environmentally imposed biases weren't enough, human nature gets a vote as well. A good number of studies in the field of decision-making have shown, "we are systematically over-confident in our own abilities."

Consider the unscientific BusinessWeek poll: "90% of managers believe they are in the top 10% of all performers in their firm."

Another annual survey is taken for incoming freshmen at Harvard, where 75% of the students believe they will end up in the top 15% of their class.

I'm all for optimism. It's most definitely a beneficial human characteristic and a likely good defense mechanism for the trials and tribulations of survival. However, it can lead us astray, sometimes in life or death situations.

The Thin Air of Life or Death Decisions:

Professor Michael Roberto in his excellent program on Critical Decision Making, uses the Everest tragedies of 1996 to showcase a myriad of decision-making errors that started with an over-confidence bias and literally cascaded downhill into a disaster from there. (Roberto's content in this segment is based on Jon Krakauer's article/book, Into Thin Air.)

As a backdrop, several of the expedition leaders in 1996 had only experienced the relatively calm conditions of the past few years on Everest. While always life threatening, the leaders had not experienced the worst of the worst and were lulled into a false sense of security by these conditions and their own recent successes in reaching the summit (a recency effect bias).

One of the expedition leaders, Scott Fischer, was quoted as saying, "*We've got the Big E completely figured out, we've got it totally wired. These days, I'm telling you, we've built a yellow brick road to the summit.*"

Another leader, Rob Hall, responding to a worried climber, offered: "*It's worked 39 times so far, pal, and a few of the blokes who summitted with me were nearly as pathetic as you.*"

Both Fischer and Hall along with six of their expedition members perished under brutal conditions made worse by a nearly unbelievable string of bad decisions.

Our Own Mountains to Climb:

While most of us aren't climbing Everest, we have our own metaphorical mountains to conquer in the form of projects, budgets, campaigns and business plans, and we're every bit as susceptible to both of the most common of estimating decision traps, the over-confidence bias and the prudence bias.

Consider:
If the management culture is one that values strict adherence to schedules and reinforces this perspective by punishing those who miss schedules, people naturally add significant padding to their estimates. For complex projects involving multiple work groups, this padding practice across all of the teams adds up to significantly longer project estimates. And let's face it, work expands to fill the time allocated for it. The cost, time-to-market (or implementation) implications are huge!

Alternatively, I've observed over-zealous executive teams declare a time-to-market mandate without consideration of the project complexities, and the pressure on the project teams results in estimates executives "want to hear," but that have no basis in the reality of the work. As time and cost estimates are missed, the environment tends to deteriorate into one of finger-pointing, excuse-making and general dysfunction.

Fear Impacts Estimates:

While fear pushes project estimates out into the future, this same environment likely results in ultra-conservative sales forecasts on one hand and unrealistic cost estimates on the other. For anyone accountable for revenue and/or expense numbers, you tend to take your cue on these numbers from environmental pressures. I've observed managers inflate revenue forecasts out of fear of being viewed as poor team players, while at the same time, arbitrarily reduce expense numbers out of fear of being viewed as not having control over costs.

Fear in the workplace creates estimating gamesmanship.

Prior Performance May Be a Poor Predictor:

Much like the recency effect displayed by the Everest expedition leaders, we open additional trap doors for our estimating and forecasting approaches by relying too much on prior performance in spite of changing conditions. The past is interesting, but in times of significant change or distress, it is a lousy predictor of future performance.

Data, Bloody Data:

We live in a data-filled world and it's common to hear management talk about the importance of making data-drive decisions. I'm all for it. After all, that's why your firm spent countless dollars and suffered through nearly endless schedule delays and cost over-runs to implement the latest business intelligence tools. However, even the best system and the cleanest data cannot compensate for our propensity as humans to seek out information that confirms our opinion and discount or discard information that doesn't. This confirming evidence trap is a frequent contributor to estimating and forecasting errors.

Six Ideas for Minimizing Estimating and Forecasting Errors:

1. Commit to improving management practices that impact estimating. If you are struggling to gain reliable project or business estimates, chances are there are systemic problems created by poor management practices. To the extent possible, you need to cultivate an estimating and forecasting culture free from fear of reprisal and low in gamesmanship. This includes eliminating practices that encourage over-confidence or extreme prudence. It also includes minimizing fear as a factor that unduly influences estimate development. The best project managers and project sponsors work hard to create a safe environment for estimate development, often serving as buffers between their working teams and the pressures coming from top management.

2. Beware the group effect. Groups tend to be over-confident, and have been shown to take larger risks and offer more aggressive estimates than individuals working on their own.

3. Seek broader data sets and encourage the introduction of information that challenges existing confirming evidence.

4. Ask for objective, 3rd party review of estimates and the assumptions underlying the estimates. High performance project teams use this approach as a safety check against groupthink and over-confidence or over-prudence. A knowledgeable but uninvolved third party can ask tough questions, challenge assumptions and indicate when estimates just don't make sense.

5. Build time for learning into estimating activities. Recognize the weakness of estimating new projects or programs based on prior results. And if you are doing something "new" and outside of the experience band of your firm, it's critical to build learning time into the process.

6. Commit to monitoring estimating performance over a period of time. Build in the process of documenting estimate assumptions, reviewing results and identifying what worked and what failed. For many teams and firms, this is a distinct process change that requires a genuine interest in improving estimating performance.

The Bottom-Line for Now:

Just about every firm and team struggles somewhere with estimating and forecasting. The root causes of these problems are found both in human nature...our propensity towards over-confidence, and in our managerial practices and their impact on the decision-making environment. Forewarned is forearmed on the human nature issue. As for the management practices, these truly are controllable by you.

Chapter 22

Beware the Tyranny of Consensus

Like bad coffee, I'm not particularly fond of leading by consensus or even seeking consensus as a decision-making tool. I've long viewed managing by consensus as a "Tyranny of Mediocrity" approach to leading and making decisions. In seeking consensus, compromises are made that eliminate the more radical, revolutionary innovations and settle on solutions that make as many parties as possible happy. Happy isn't always right!

M y callous and perhaps bad-coffee fueled statement on my cold-hearted approach to consensus is that I don't care if you are happy or unhappy about a key decision or direction. Your happiness, while nice, is your own responsibility, not mine as the leader, when it comes to running the business.

Ouch!

The right decisions often leave entire groups of individuals uncomfortable, because those decisions fly in the face of convention, demand change and often require the development of new skills.

General Eisenhower sought consensus on his decision to launch the D-Day offensive that ultimately led to victory for the allies in Europe. The lousy weather meant that logistics would be tough and more men would die. However, the window was closing for timing and the ability to maintain the element of surprise. Eisenhower's generals were evenly split and it was up to him as the leader to make the call that would change the fates of so many individuals and nations. "We'll go," were his reported words as he stared out the window into the fog that was to complicate the day.

Now before you slam this book shut in annoyance with my seemingly cold, callous and slightly arrogant view on decision-making, at least consider that I didn't encourage you to ignore individual or group opinions. On the contrary, as the leader, it is your job to "seek first to understand" before you "seek to be understood." Still, at the end of the day, for some issues, you must stare into the fog and decide on your own, in spite of your imperfect knowledge and the potential downsides of your decision. Relying on consensus may just prove too costly.

The Bottom-Line for Now:

I've watched and participated as an effective leader worked hard to understand the problem and the many ideas on resolving that problem. I've also respected as that leader ultimately opted for a direction he believed was the "right" choice, not the "popular" choice. And while I preferred my idea, I respected this leader, and as a good follower, it was now my job to wholeheartedly support the decision.

First-time leaders often make the mistake of assuming that they need to make everyone on their team happy by adopting a consensus style. I've observed this approach carried over into mid-career and even in some cases, used by senior executives. It has always struck me as an approach that is OK for the small stuff and horribly wrong for the big calls that rest on the shoulders of leaders. Don't let the Tyranny of Mediocrity be your legacy.

Section 4

Problems? Try Looking in the Mirror for a Change

I n the section *on Developing Yourself*, I encourage you to work hard to learn to, "see yourself as others see you." One of the core lessons from working hard to develop a more objective view of yourself is the recognition that some of the problems you face on a daily basis have their roots in your own leadership practices.

Earlier in my career, I was convinced that I needed to change everyone to my view and to my way of doing things. It took some time and a few hard knocks over the head for me to recognize I was fighting the wrong battle. My job was to form and frame the right workplace atmosphere for people to leverage their own skills and strengths in pursuit of achieving our goals. Instead of fighting, I worked harder to support my team. Instead of telling people what to do, I started teaching. And, instead of pushing my view of the world, I began to appreciate how the views of others aligned with and supported the pursuit of our mission. The results improved tremendously once I quit being the problem.

Chapter 23

At Least Twenty Things to Quit Doing as a Leader

We spend a lot of time teaching our leaders what to do.
We don't spend enough time teaching them what to stop."
-Peter Drucker

Here's my small contribution on what to "stop doing" immediately.

20 Things to Stop Doing as a Leader (in no particular order):

1. Stop barking orders at people like you're a drill instructor.

2. Stop expecting people to read your mind.

3. Stop making people feel like taking time off to go on vacation is a sin.

4. Stop multi-tasking when someone asks you a question.

5. Stop handing out only the negative feedback.

6. Stop dressing down people in public.

7. Stop saving all of your feedback for the annual performance review.

8. Stop letting people wander through their days with no context for the organization's strategic priorities.

9. Stop ignoring people that you don't like.

10. Stop showing that you don't like people.

11. Stop reminding everyone that you are the boss.

12. Stop taking credit for the work of others.

13. Stop playing favorites.

14. Stop making everything "all about you."

15. Stop forgetting to provide people with fresh challenges.

16. Stop worrying about what your team members are saying to their co-workers about you. On second thought, maybe you should worry.

17. Stop declaring everything a crisis.

18. Stop blocking our access to people in other groups.

19. Stop managing by fear and intimidation.

20. Stop hoarding information on company and team performance.

The Bottom-Line for Now:

If you're a boss, see the list above and just stop it!

Chapter 24

Quit Managing Reduced Expectations

I set expectations for my teams and team members very high.
I have yet to be disappointed.

A great friend and talented product manager once offered in a moment of frustration that he viewed his principal job as one of "managing reduced expectations."

This brilliant, but depressing turn of words reflected bigger business problems, including a logjam in development that effectively precluded us from doing anything to enhance the competitiveness of our products in a timeframe shorter than something you might find on a geological time-scale.

The "managing reduced expectations" seems to be a theme inherent in our society right now. Spiraling debt, a never-ending string of mortgage defaults, long-lingering unemployment, embattled and embittered government, corruption, a seeming shift of the balance of economic and productive power away from North America, and potentially unsolvable geopolitical issues are all contributors to this collective mood referenced in the media and heard on the street daily. Throw in a few good old-fashioned ecological and natural disasters and some remarkable leadership letdowns during the past decade, and the process of managing reduced expectations is now epidemic.

It's remarkably easy to let the broader environmental factors and forces dictate our personal emotions and before we know it, an attitude of blind resignation sets in and dominates our thinking and our actions.

A Few "Reduced Expectations" Phrases that Annoy Me:

- *We see a huge opportunity for our new product; however, corporate is telling us that we can't invest in the brainpower that we need to take advantage of the opportunity.*

- *Times are tough and we're not going to pursue this project this year.*

- *We're not running leadership training anymore. We killed that in this year's budget planning.*

What the Hell Are You Doing?

Sorry for the strong title on this section, but again, "What the hell?" You're telling me that you are going to take it lying down while your future is decided by someone wielding the expense-cutting sword to hit arbitrary targets?

You're not pursuing a project that will define your future and perhaps change the course of your firm, because no one is working hard enough to cull the portfolio or find the money. And you gave up developing your people because why?

The Bottom-Line for Now:

In the words of Red Foreman on television's *That 70's Show,* "Dumb Asses."

It's time to quit managing reduced expectations. There's a big, troubled world out there filled with emerging markets and new consumers hungry for basics and then eventually, luxuries. Of course, to seize opportunities here and abroad, you've got to jettison old ways, take risks that might have seemed incomprehensible yesterday, and work unceasingly on surrounding yourself with people that can-do and don't allow dumb-ass reasons to get in the way. The change starts with you. Start managing towards high-expectations and find every way possible to reinforce great behavior, reward successes and build enthusiasm.

Chapter 25

For a Change, Look at What's Working

What's your view on the world? Do you see the gaps and flaws in everything, or, do you see the beauty and what's right about the image or situation you are viewing? How you see things directly impacts your leadership style and the affect that you have on those around you.

Or, "Clark, your Italian twinkling lights aren't twinkling." "I know Arthur, and thanks for pointing that out." –paraphrased from the movie Christmas Vacation *with Chevy Chase.*

Consider these common refrains from two different leaders looking at the same issue:

Positive Leader: *"That's great! Congratulations! How do we do more of that?"*

Negative Leader: *"We got lucky on that project. Let's look at all the things we did wrong."*

We've all met both of these leaders. One sees opportunity, achievement and building blocks everywhere she looks and the other sees flaws and problems that need fixing. And while you are free to accuse me of making a hasty generalization here, my "blink" assessment of the two is that I want to hire or work for the Positive Leader.

Don't get me wrong. I like the attitude of the Negative Leader if we're talking about toilets, sump pumps and just about anything else that is found in the plumbing family. Otherwise, Positive is my choice for manager or project leader.

I'm not certain why some see beauty and what's right in people and things, and others see gaps and flaws when looking at the same objects. In the world of leadership, I do worry that some of this reflects bad habits carried forward from early, unsupervised and un-coached first-time leadership roles. More than a few first-time leaders are thrown or drafted into their positions with no more of an idea of what to do than you or I might have if we were asked to perform surgery today. Without proper guidance and training, the instinct to "tell" or to "order" kicks in as a survival response.

And yes, you continuous improvement disciples might appropriately chastise me for discrediting the person that's looking for things to continuously improve. My focus here is on the impact that these two different leaders have on the people around them. Positive fuels performance by encouraging people to build on successes and Negative flummoxes people by going for the negatives or the gaps. Positive's style not only doesn't preclude continuous improvement, I believe it fuels it by reinforcing the notion of doing more of "what's working."

I've worked for both of these characters at different points during my career, and now I see them regularly in my client assignments. The results are always the same:

- Positive's teams are productive and creative, and good people migrate towards this leader.

- Negative's teams are often efficient but lifeless. Good people seek to escape and those that don't mind the constant "here's what's wrong" view of the world, linger on, comfortable in the fact that someone will tell them what to fix.

Five Ideas For Changing Your View from What's Wrong to What's Right:

1. Project post-mortems are a great place to start. Instead of the typical, "let's assess what we did wrong and how we can improve next time," try: "what did we do right and how can we do more of it next time?" I guarantee two very different conversations.

2. Set a goal every day to offer one piece of behavioral, business-focused positive feedback every hour. Keep tally of how well you do. And remember, the feedback has to be genuine, specific and behavioral enough that someone will understand what to keep doing or to do more of. A classic example is, "nice presentation." It's fine to hear that, but what did you do that was nice? A more specific example might be, "during your presentation, you really engaged the audience. Your eye-contact was excellent, your body posture was open and inviting, and best of all, your constant smile warmed everyone up."

3. Bite your tongue and hold-off every time you are tempted to criticize. While I don't want you to short-circuit your use of constructive feedback, I do want you to quit telling everyone what's wrong, what's not working and what needs to be fixed. Replace statements with questions and then shut up and listen!

4. Try adjusting your altitude to a level above the treetops and start consciously looking at the big picture of what your team does effectively. Let them know how impressed you are by their work and their outcomes.

5. Let your team members find the areas that need to be improved upon, and then encourage them to take ownership of those ideas. Take it a step further and help knock down some obstacles so that they succeed with their improvement initiatives.

The Bottom-Line for Now:

Don't think for a second that I'm asking you to walk around and avoid dealing with problems. I am, however, encouraging you to adjust your focus a bit and start looking at something other than what's wrong. If you already do this, do more of it. And if you're reading this saying, "that's not me," it can't hurt to try the above suggestions, can it?

Here's to building on strengths and successes. And here's to plumbers everywhere that keep the water flowing and toilets draining!

Chapter 26

Mistakes are the Raw Ingredients of Leadership Courage

I've made a number of mistakes over the course of my leadership career that make my head spin and my stomach turn just thinking about them. No life or death or business impacting mistakes, but, definitely some people and team impacting issues that created ill will and most definitely didn't show me off at my leadership best. Learning from those mistakes helped me evolve my thinking on the role of a leader and on my true priorities in supporting my business, my peers and my team members. While it would have been nice to skip these speed bumps, the lessons are forever burned into my memory.

Somewhere along the road to making my share of mistakes, an interesting thing happened to my fear of making mistakes. It disappeared! And don't misinterpret my statement. I don't seek out mistakes and I don't not (double negative by design) care about mistakes, but, I just don't fear them. In fact, I'm more concerned about not riding on the cutting edge of what I believe to be the right thing for my stakeholders than I am about falling off and getting shredded in the process.

A leader preoccupied with the fear of making a mistake is playing not to lose versus playing to win. It turns out that developing personal courage is critical to developing as an effective leader.

Six Situations Where A Leader's Courage is Critical:

1. Doing the right thing promptly and fairly when it comes to dealing with performance issues, including screwing up the courage to deliver tough feedback every day.

2. Accepting accountability for your mistakes and for your team's mistakes or performance lapses.

3. Supporting the person you truly believe in, regardless of prevailing opinions.

4. Supporting a person that you believe in, in spite of the fact that she may not believe in herself.

5. Advocating a direction that challenges the traditional thinking (Prahalad's "dominant logic") while taking direct hits from the slings and arrows of, "We've never done it that way before."

6. Learning to say "no" to people and projects for the right reasons. "No," may be the toughest word to learn in the leader's vocabulary.

The Bottom-Line for Now:

You'll make more than a few mistakes, and if you're committed to developing as an effective leader, you'll learn to quickly seize the learning opportunities, adjust your course as needed and move on to better performance. Here's to our mistakes!

Chapter 27

Too Much Time with the Wrong People

My biggest mistakes as a leader occurred as a result of spending too much time attempting to change two people. I was young and new to the formal leadership scene and was convinced that with my help and guidance, these two talented individuals would certainly shed their dysfunctional and toxic behaviors. Wow, was I wrong!

After a lot of time, money, coaching, counseling and training, one lawsuit and one person storming out never to be seen again, along with untold amounts of collateral damage to the team and my own credibility as a leader, I had learned my lesson. People do not fundamentally change their nature.

I've been accused of sounding cynical and jaded as a result of my own early misfires, and perhaps I am. Nonetheless, I learned in a painful way why I needed to hire slowly and fire fast. I've been well served incorporating this approach since learning those painful lessons.

In workshop settings, I present appropriately sanitized versions of those now two-decade old cases and it is fascinating to watch people make my same mistakes over and over again. Without getting into too much detail, both cases involve talented individuals who create havoc on teams through their approaches. They are toxic, but they are both so freaking talented at their jobs, that it is easy for people and their manager to excuse their behaviors. "That's just Bob," or "That's just Suzy." In essence, the manager and those around them become their enablers and excusers.

After reviewing the cases and debating "what to do" in small groups, I invariably get these responses:
"Create a new position"
"Put him/her in a different role"
"More coaching"

Almost no one suggests firing the individuals until I play the devil's advocate.

The unfortunate reality is that many managers are unprepared to deal with the "brilliant problem-child" character and they fall victim to the same fate as the erstwhile frog in the *"Parable of the Scorpion and the Frog."* In case you haven't heard it: Scorpion needs a ride across a pond and asks the frog to carry him over on his back. Frog at first says, "No, you'll sting me and we'll both die and what purpose would that serve? Scorpion says, "No I won't, I've changed." Frog thinks about it for a while, says, "OK, jump on." The frog starts swimming across the pond, gets halfway, the scorpion stings him and as he's going down, he asks, "Why did you do that?" The Scorpion responds, "I can't help it, it's my nature."

The Bottom-Line for Now:

You cannot change people. They have to want to change and unfortunately, deep, lasting and significant change is rare indeed. Like the scorpion above, people don't change their nature. You are in danger of spending too much time with the wrong people. Cut it out. Focus on those that are striving to learn and grow.

Hire very, very slowly and fire fast. You'll make fewer critical mistakes this way.

Chapter 28

Five Simple Suggestions for Minimizing Management Myopia

Participate in or monitor enough management team conversations and you will invariably conclude that it's darned hard for these teams to spend quality time discussing external issues. The gravitational pull of internal "stuff" is overwhelming and resists all attempts to move the conversation to topics outside of the firm's four walls, preferring instead to keep managers focused on the nuances of their own operations. The result is self-fulfilling management myopia where the view on the world is grossly limited to the immediate surroundings.

Myopic firms miss market moves and focus incorrectly on improving yesterday's systems, products and services while customers are looking and moving forward in search of new solutions to emerging vexing problems.

Overcoming management myopia requires extraordinary effort on the part of key leaders to train and enable their teams to move outside of the four walls and to build a more comprehensive market view that is constantly in the process of being refreshed.

Five Simple Suggestions for Minimizing Management Myopia:

1. Conduct outside-in meetings. Start by scheduling regular forums where the only items discussed are external in nature. Create a series of core questions that challenge team members to show up prepared to talk about what's going on with customers, competitors and other industry ecosystem players. Resist the urge in these forums to move towards actions and internal items. Focus on: "What does this mean for our customers?"

2. Translate external and customer issues into something more than hot air and wasted time. Teach your team members to end their discussions of external forces/factors/changes with *"What this means for our firm is... ."* Capture these notes.

3. Get everyone involved in monitoring the external environment. Charge team members with the task of monitoring specific competitors and industry participants and providing regular updates to the group as well as instantaneous updates as conditions change. Remember, the insights must always be accompanied by, "What this means for our firm is..." statements. Rotate assignments periodically to keep people fresh.

4. Observe and interview customers often. It's interesting to sit around and speculate about what customers are doing or thinking, but it's much more compelling and actionable to truly understand what's on their minds. Again, create a simple customer survey script and charge your key managers and contributors with keeping tabs on specific customers. I've done this with development resources, product managers and executive managers, and it gets people on your team connected to someone in the market. And remember, when visiting customers, observations may be as important or more important than their answers to your questions. Bring the findings into your "external forums" and share.

5. Even if you only operate inside your firm's walls, recognize that you have customers. If your team is internally focused such as IT or an internal support group, make certain to forge relationships with external facing colleagues and departments. Invite members of these groups to join your meetings and to share updates on current market issues. Pay attention for opportunities to better tune your function's activities and address priorities to issues and opportunities that your external facing colleagues see in the market.

The Bottom-Line for Now:

Inevitably the best outcome of good external awareness is the reflection of insights in program, product and service improvements that create value for customers and profitable growth for your firm. You will need to develop a good mechanism for translating external awareness into internal execution, however, that's an essay for another day. For now, set a goal to increase your team's External IQ and try the suggestions here on for size.

Chapter 29
Give Your People Room to Run

Overheard: "If I don't stay on top of my people, nothing gets done."

I f lousy leadership were a crime, the owner of the quote above might just merit a short stretch of quality alone time to reflect on the implications of his statement. There are so many things truly wrong with the style of leadership that the statement connotes, that I'm not certain where to start.

I regularly run into examples of leaders operating on the frontlines and the top-lines that equate leading with policing and oversight. In sessions where I poll on the behaviors of great and lousy leaders, the horror stories of micro-managing bosses and inspector and critic style managers are so plentiful that it's often difficult to rein in the discussions. The perception that being a boss involves constant policing has not yet been bred out of our culture.

There are certainly core issues that demand oversight. Issues of ethics, legal compliance, and discrimination all merit constant vigilance. And maintaining appropriate operational control is absolutely a leader's responsibility. However, there's a line that is crossed when the boss extends intense vigilance to the day-to-day and sometimes minute-to-minute work effort of team members. Move too close to this line, and you guarantee a tense working atmosphere, a loss of initiative and a deficit of creativity.

Gaining compliance is not leading. Any two-bit despot can gain compliance by inducing fear through excessive oversight. In conversations with individuals describing leaders they admire, the commonly described behaviors are the exact opposite of what you've come to expect from the overbearing and over-the-shoulder manager. I hear statements such as:

She doesn't micromanage me.
He lets me do my job.
She always asks me how she can help.
He sets clear expectations and then lets me do my thing.
She doesn't jump all over me when I make a mistake.

These all reflect leadership maturity and confidence, and they communicate respect and trust. Simple words with a big impact!

9 Reminders that Your Priorities Are About Building, Not Guarding:

1. You own the responsibility to create and sustain a positive working environment. You cannot do that by micromanaging.

2. You are a teacher. Teach and train. And then teach some more.

3. You are a coach. Observe and provide timely constructive AND positive feedback. Every day.

4. You must be approachable, but don't spend all of your own time approaching. Give your team room to run.

5. You own the task of providing context for your organization's strategies and goals. Clarify and communicate.

6. Always set clear and challenging expectations for individual and team performance. This is not micromanaging. It is good management.

7. Focus on helping, not hindering progress. Knock down obstacles and free your people to run.

8. Defend, don't distract. Learn to shield team members from distractions.

9. Stay out of the way. You are a distraction most of the time. See the prior item.

The Bottom-Line for Now:

Much like parenting, good leading is all about setting the stage to "let go." It's sometimes counter-intuitive and it's often difficult, but at the end of the day, it is critically important. Give your people some room to run and they will surprise you.

Section 5

The Nimble Leader

I really like the word "nimble" when it comes to describing today's successful leaders. "Quick and light in movement...quick to comprehend...intellectually nimble." While this old English word may not be something you hear or use on a daily basis, it captures the essence of what a leader needs to be to survive the onslaught of issues, opportunities, decision-choices and people and project dilemmas we face constantly.

Some of my favorite nimble leaders are product and project managers. Good product and project managers are worth their weight in gold. They get stuff done and their work directly affects strategy execution. They have the toughest jobs in the organization...a ton of accountability and responsibility, yet, very little formal leadership authority. All of their leadership authority is earned the hard way...by building trust and respect with individuals in all areas of the organizations. If you want to see some nimble leaders, seek out a well-respected project or product manager as a mentor. Watch and learn.

The essays in this section offer encouragement and guidance for navigating sticky situations, coping with ambiguity, cultivating key skills, surviving life in the middle of the organization and a few more. Read carefully and apply liberally.

Chapter 30

If You Are Walking on Eggshells, Something is Wrong

While it's doubtful that many of us have ever literally attempted to walk on egg-shells, the phrase is idiomatic for those situations where we are fearful of confront-ing or even engaging with someone, lest we draw their attention or raise their ire. I reference these individuals as Attitude Bullies.

Overheard from Various Managers:

"I have to walk on eggshells around her."
"He's volatile, and I don't want to upset him, so I steer clear and let him do his thing."
"I'm afraid to confront her."
"He's too valuable to the firm, so we all kind of look the other way."

How Much Energy are You Expending Trying to Walk on Eggshells?

As an early career leader, I recall one individual who masterfully exuded dis-dain and annoyance every time I approached him. Whether it was real or just an act to keep the boss away, it worked until I recognized that I could not do my job while ignoring this character.

I've observed as other individuals have allowed toxic employees to manipulate team and office dynamics by creating an "aura of fear" to keep people in check. And in what may be the most commonplace of all situations, many leaders excuse the behavior of these characters by rationalizing the situation. "He's the best at (insert activity), and we can't afford to lose him." If you can relate to any of the situations above, or, if you have your own special Attitude Bully that you find yourself "walking on eggshells" for, it's time solve this problem. *(Note: my focus here is on situations where your primary fear is, "fear of reaction." If you sense fear of physical reprisal, stop reading and engage your manager and HR department immediately.)*

Six Ideas for Clearing Away the Eggshells and Coping with Attitude Bullies:

1. Engage. Your instinct is to avoid and ignore. Do the opposite. You need to cultivate a formal relationship with the individual in question. Without engaging fairly and professionally with the Attitude Bully, you have no behavioral basis for feedback, coaching or ultimately, some form of discipline, including termination.

2. Clarify Accountability. The Attitude Bully understands that his/her approach results in different standards for accountability compared to the broader population. You need to eliminate any opportunity for a double standard by clarifying the individual's responsibility for results. The results include actual outcomes as well as process and engagement quality. One manager used post-project performance evaluations from team members and the project manager to facilitate discussions on interpersonal approach, attitude and other behaviors. Regardless of approach, the Attitude Bully must understand what they are accountable for in terms of results and workplace behaviors.

3. Observe Often, Reinforce Positives and Tackle Negatives. Neither the Attitude Bully nor anyone around you will take you seriously until you hold this person accountable for their results and for their behavior. The best way to manage this situation is to observe the individual's work with others as much as possible. If the individual is a true individual contributor without much team involvement, it's all on your shoulders to engage often enough to offer quality, behavioral feedback. Tackle performance issues immediately and provide positive feedback as long as it is merited.

4. Warning! Don't Apologize or Attempt to Praise Your Way Forward. It takes time for some managers to overcome their fear of Attitude Bullies, and those initial steps to engage are awkward and even frightening for some. Beware the tendency to engage by apologizing for your intrusion, and resist the urge to offer positive praise for behaviors that simply meet the standards that everyone else is accountable for. You only weaken your case with the Attitude Bully when he observes your visible discomfort via false praise or excessive apologizing.

5. Build on Progress. More than a few Attitude Bullies have responded to appropriate attention from the boss by becoming productive members of the workplace environment. While I'm practicing psychology without a license on this one, I suspect that some behaviors are cries for attention and for respect. Your willingness to pay attention to someone is a powerful motivator. As you observe positive progress, offer appropriate feedback and importantly, test the relationship by extending your trust on workplace responsibilities. Assuming that your trust is rewarded with results, keep it going.

6. Cut Your Losses. There's a managerial due diligence process (different than a formal HR process) when it comes to dealing with Attitude Bullies. Your intent going into the "adjustment" process should not be to fire, but to help. Follow the guidelines above, provide clear feedback, document your interactions, and look for progress.

At the end of the day, if you are doing your job as a manager, your involvement will neutralize and even help the individual reform, or, you will have the basis for moving down the path of purging this workplace toxin. Ultimately, your issue is not about attitude, but rather about dealing with performance issues. You've got to engage to manage.

The Bottom-Line for Now:

Too many managers spend too much time walking on eggshells. They either avoid the Attitude Bullies or, they deal with them in a manner that reinforces aberrant behaviors. You're much better suited to sweep the eggshells out of the way and engage to either build a better relationship or establish the basis for ending the relationship. Don't be afraid to reach out for help from a mentor. Your only mistake here is to continue to try and defy physics and walk across the eggshells. You'll crush something along the way, and it may be your future prospects in your firm.

Chapter 31

Embrace Ambiguity and Grow with It

During many years of leading others, I've worked hard to help people think for themselves in circumstances clouded by ambiguity. Coping with increasing levels of ambiguity is a part of developing as a senior contributor.

There are ample opportunities every day for you to reinforce the lesson that people need to make decisions for themselves instead of seeking you out for the answers. Consider the following exchanges:

Employee: *"What do you think I should do?"*

Me: *"I don't know, what do you think?"*

Or:

Employee: *"How do you want the presentation formatted?"*

Me: *"Format it so that it clearly communicates your key points."*

Or (same person, now exasperated):

Employee: *"How many pages should the report be?"*

Me: *"I don't know. How many will it take to concisely and clearly communicate your key points?"*

Or, my favorite:

Employee: *"What should we do?"*

Me: *"I'm going to go get a cup of coffee. What are you going to do?"*

These questions come from students and employees, and I'm willing to bet that you hear variations of these from time to time as well. Our inclination is to show our expertise by offering up answers or even by doing the work in some cases. Trust me, everyone is better served if you politely encourage people to decide for themselves.

The reality is, many people fear ambiguity and/or they don't trust their own ability to create or solve a problem, so they respond with a question that delegates the thinking to someone else. They lack self-confidence, or, they fear being called-out for doing something that doesn't meet with the boss's approval. That's a bad habit, and if the workplace or college classrooms were refereed events, those "you do my thinking for me so I don't have to be creative or take a risk" questions would be infractions.

A Classroom Lesson Learned in Coping with Ambiguity:

One of my own favorite lessons in ambiguity occurred a few years ago in an executive workshop at Kellogg. It was day one of the program on "Reinventing Leadership," and a group of executives ranging from Director to CEO had just concluded presenting the results of our first breakout and case. I noticed that the dual instructors were fairly critical of the less than creative problem-solving and uninspired presentations, and after some coaching with an edge, they proceeded to the next case. We broke back out into our work groups and came back in the room to run the teach-backs, and this is where everything changed.

After the first few report-backs, the instructors quit responding. They sat there and glowered at the room in silence. No other groups were called and you can imagine the fidgeting and palpable increase in tension in the room.

Several people tried asking questions and were met with stern, stone-faced glares.

After what seemed like an eternity, one CEO stood up and said, "This is B.S., I've got better things to do," and grabbed his papers and jacket and started to leave. Another participant stopped him and said, "Let's figure this out...don't let these guys beat you." That statement was the turning point.

Slowly people came to life and recognized that we were being played... deservedly so, for delivering uninspiring solutions to vexing issues in our cases, and that the message here was dig deeper and do better. Instead of reverting to our prior work groups, a new social order emerged with several people taking charge, organizing work teams, clarifying the problems and objectives and others joined in to facilitate solutions. Before you know it, the room was humming with creativity as the instructors continued glaring at no one in particular. Basically, we ignored them.

The exercise continued as each new work group presented suggestions and through another round of integration of ideas, we came up with what we all agreed was an inspired, novel set of do-able solutions for the problems at hand. No instructor involvement required. Now it was our turn. We all sat down and silently stared back at the instructors. And finally, they broke their vow of silence with big grins, apologies and their heartfelt praise. The lessons were powerful and plentiful from that example, not the least of which was how to turn brutal, crushing ambiguity (the silence) into a creative outcome. This week long program continued with other powerful exercises, but none that left such a strong impression as the few hours of silence.

The Bottom-Line for Now:

Whether you are a leader or a contributor, recognize that ambiguity is an invitation to pursue creativity. If you are fortunate enough to work for a boss who encourages freethinking and that doesn't mandate explicit compliance on tasks, take advantage of this environment to see what you are capable of creating. If you are the manager, quit answering these questions and teach people to think for themselves.

One of the joys of working is the opportunity to create and the benefits derived from the powerful learning experiences that accrue in the process. Quit asking, start thinking and you'll surprise yourself.

Chapter 32

When Leading from the Middle, Be The Example

I've observed or participated in countless scenarios where much needed organizational change started somewhere in the middle and spread like wildfire, catching top management by pleasant surprise. Alternatively, sitting around and complaining about what's wrong is a favorite pastime of many managers and a company-wide activity in some organizations. You have the choice to sit idly by and join the complainers, or, to take initiative and be the example.

I love it during presentations and workshops when an audience member steps up and makes a point that helps tie everything together with a concrete example.

I recently found myself as a guest speaker in a good-natured discussion with my audience about the challenges that mid-level managers face in trying to facilitate positive culture change while working in a toxic or at least a less than ideal work environment. I opt for the affirmative in this debate, and often find myself arguing the minority opinion.

I absolutely have strong convictions about the ability of one individual or a small group of individuals to catalyze positive environmental change in the most challenging of environments. In spite of my best "glass is more than half-full, you can make a difference, build an island of competence in a sea of insanity pitches," I sensed from the audience reaction that I was once again on the minority side of this one.

Before describing how an audience member came to my aid and helped turn a smiling but unruly (on this point) crowd around, some background is in order. Every semester, I am invited to serve as a guest speaker for a course on Creative Leadership, where my book with Rich Petro, *Practical Lessons in Leadership*, is one of the two featured course texts.

I love this event. It is incredibly gratifying to walk into a room of adult learners and see the book in front of everyone, a bit dog-eared and usually with post-its sticking out from between the pages. And while that's great, the real thrill comes from engaging with a group of sharp professionals that have spent the past few weeks dissecting the words and leadership concepts that Rich and I labored over a few years ago. Some agree whole-heartedly and others have been waiting to see me and are loaded for bear with questions and the occasional difference of opinion.

I know from experience that the topic of, "What's a person to do in a tough environment?" will come up every time. Well-intentioned people want to make a difference, but often hold back out of fear or a sense of futility or a combination of the two. In this particular instance, the discussion had progressed for a few minutes and one young woman raised her hand and said something to the effect of, "We did this at my workplace, and while it took time, after several years of working at it from the middle, we have a very different culture now."

She went on to describe how in a toxic workplace where top leadership seemed to be disengaged, a number of the middle managers got together and decided to start shaping a culture that was decidedly more positive than the current one. They started by agreeing that it was their responsibility as managers to begin acting and leading in a way that set a positive example for everyone around them. Over time, and with reinforcement, the changes took hold and the working environment evolved into one where teams and individuals focused on learning and achieving.

Great stuff, and if nothing else, she offered hope to the people in the room that want to make a difference, but aren't sure it's a fight worth fighting or one that they could win. I would have loved to have spent more time learning about the details of culture transition, but we ran out of time. Nonetheless, the issue for today is not so much the mechanics that moved the culture from toxic to positive, but the fact that it did and that it can. In essence, the managers looked in the mirror and recognized that for meaningful change to take place, the responsibility was on their shoulders to set the right example. Instead of complaining or endlessly commiserating with each other, they took it upon themselves to act.

The Bottom-Line for Now:

Be the Example. Our words as leaders are just empty utterances unless we truly show and lead by example. Start this week and renew your commitment to effective, people-focused and values-based leadership and be the example that you want generations behind you to follow and aspire to as they develop as leaders.

Treat people with respect. Start by adjusting your priorities to focus on issues of support and substance versus the banal details that rule so much of our professional lives. Things go wrong every day, and today and from this point forward, remind yourself that the height of a problem is the best opportunity for you to lead by example. Resist the urge to shoot first and ask later. Turn these into teaching and developmental opportunities by helping others step up and take their swing at fixing and improving.

As you walk through the door, shift your focus from one of, "I'm here," to, "I'm glad you're here." Believe me, everyone will notice.

And as you walk out the door at night, reflect back on the example that you set during this precious day and vow to do better tomorrow. And then come back and live up to your vow.

Chapter 33

Four Signs that Your Leadership Approach is Working

Most leaders struggle to understand whether they are helping or hindering the cause. Except, of course, for those leaders/narcissists who believe that their every utterance is sheer genius wrapped in pure motivational gold.

How do you know if what you are doing as a leader is working? The feedback from your manager, while important, tends to be based on either numbers or casual observation. And feedback from your team members is welcomed, but you never really know for sure whether it's the unvarnished type.

The "Am I Helping?" issue is particularly important when a troubled team gains a fresh leader. I've lived this situation a number of times and I've spoken with leaders familiar with navigating the throes of turnarounds and significant change initiatives about how they measure their own effectiveness. Most agree that while the indicators of progress and personal effectiveness aren't posted on the wall every day, the signs are present in the workplace for everyone to read.

Whether overtly or through their interpersonal and working dynamics, it turns out that your team members make it pretty clear whether you are helping, hindering or just taking up space, time and valuable oxygen.

However, it's up to you as the leader to learn to read these important and often subtle signs and to adjust accordingly.

4 Signs that Your Leadership Approach is Working:

1. The quality of the conversations improves. Most troubled teams or organizations struggle to create high-quality conversations that focus on facts, tough issues and that sort through ideas, opinions and options. Often, the dialogue reflects denial or it unduly preoccupies on the negatives in the situation. Effective leaders help conversations move in the right direction by creating an environment of transparency and candor. Easy words, but a difficult task that takes time and a nearly constant care and feeding by the leader.

2. Idea flow increases. An important by-product of improved conversation quality is the increased flow of ideas for fixing today's problems and ideas for creating the future. Troubled teams led by lousy leaders are conditioned to focus on what's in front of them at the expense of ignoring the big picture. Alternatively, effective leaders recognize that the one and only way to create the future is to leverage the collective grey-matter of the team. These leaders look for the flow of ideas to start as a trickle and end up as a torrent. Things are working when ideas begin to turn into actions.

3. Collaboration occurs. Troubled teams with disgruntled team members struggle to work together. It's common for these teams to fail to translate squabbling into anything resembling constructive output. However, groups on the mend tend to rediscover the fun and power of working together, and what was just recently a "No Collaboration Zone" begins to look and act like an environment that recognizes that people are interdependent upon one another.

4. Pride returns and quality breaks out all over. The shift from an unhealthy environment where people do what they are told to a situation where personal pride drives individual and group accountability for quality is a powerful sign that a leader's approach is fostering the right results. Effective execution becomes important to the group and the pursuit of high-performance moves from lofty words to tangible goals. This tends to be a longer-range lagging indicator than several of the others and as it kicks in, the leader must recognize that his/her job is to increasingly emphasize knocking down obstacles and supporting the emergence of new leaders in the workplace.

The Bottom-Line for Now:

Effective leaders understand that the measures described above are important outcomes of a great deal of hard work and not just random accidents. Effective leaders gauge their own progress by the visibility and trends of these measures more than by the traditional measures of performance or the often slightly (or majorly) biased input of managers and team members. Get these right and top and bottom-line improvements flow.

While there are no gauges to precisely indicate the barometric pressure changes created by your approach to leading, awareness of and sensitivity to these measures is an important starting point.

Chapter 34

Scouting for Talent in Unusual Places

A friend on Twitter offered up this quote as an old Turkish proverb, apropos for the weekly Leadership Caffeine article: "Coffee should be black as hell, strong as death and sweet as love." If that doesn't stimulate some senses, nothing will!

The focus here is on scouting talent, and like most of my articles, I'm encouraging you to break some established rules in pursuit of excellence.

The best leaders I know are also the best talent scouts. They are acute observers of people and extraordinarily quick to identify individuals with potential. They are also great developers of talent, but that's a separate topic for another day.

Talent Scouts in Action:

- There's the sales manager who never visited a city without setting up meetings with prospective future reps. He was so good at building a pipeline of talented professionals interested in working for him, that whenever there was an opening in his region, the position was filled immediately. His region was number one in the company year after year.

- In another case, a corporate executive watched in fascination as a young retail employee in a cell phone store calmed angry customers while fixing their problems and simultaneously helping his less capable associates with their customer issues. He was not the manager, but clearly, he was the leader on the floor. The executive shared how impressed that he was with the young clerk, passed along a business card and asked him to call. Fast forward several years and this former cell store clerk is now a top partner relations director for one of the world's largest tech firms.

- A marketing manager had an uncanny ability for identifying college interns with great potential. His batting average was 1,000 when he recommended that an intern be hired for a full-time position upon graduation. In all cases, those interns went on to become remarkable contributors.

What Great Talent Scouts Look For:

In my experience working around and leading great talent scouts, I've discovered talking with that there are typically three core attributes they look for in people:

1. Character: Top scouts recognize that they can teach and help hone skills, and teach industry and position particulars, but they know that they cannot teach character. This is a deal breaker regardless of potential.

2. Passion: Similar to character, you cannot teach someone to be passionate about fielding angry customer issues with enthusiasm and pride. Talent scouts look for people that put their heart into their work, regardless of how mundane or difficult it may be.

3. Raw Talent: The executive who shared the cell-phone clerk example above indicated that he is often able to envision someone several years down the road applying his or her natural skills to new problems in very different environments. "The ability to make angry people happy, while supporting colleagues and compensating for a weak manager were all transferrable to managing complex partner relationships," he indicated.

Five Ideas for Honing Your Talent Scouting Skills:

1. Make it your mission. Accept that one of your most critical functions is to ensure a steady flow of great talent on to your team and into your organization.

2. Listen and observe in meetings and company events. The next great product manager might be laboring in engineering testing or the next great sales representative might be working in customer support.

3. Expand your talent-scouting horizon. Move through the world with the idea that your server in a restaurant or the retail clerk helping you in the cell phone store might be a great future contributor.

4. Tap into people's passion for their work. Learn to ask questions that allow people to showcase their character and passion. A key to this is learning to be quiet. Quit talking and listen hard.

5. Learn to see people through your future vision. Are the habits and skills on display today transferrable to future challenges in different circumstances and settings?

The Bottom-Line for Now:

Who said that the best hires have to come through traditional means? I take pride in finding great talent in unusual places. Frankly, I would rather cultivate my high performance team by blending individuals from diverse backgrounds and experience sets.

Our traditional HR models teach us to hire clones or to reach out for people that don't exist. We either hire from our competitors or we specify insanely detailed job descriptions that few fit and then fool ourselves into believing that because someone looks and feels like that job description, they will succeed. Baloney!

Hone your talent scouting skills, broaden your horizons and yes, take what will look to your firm's hiring administrators as a few more risks. Ultimately, the only risk is whether or not you are up to supporting the development of your diverse and talented team members.

Chapter 35

An Effective Leader's Resolutions are Calendar Blind

For the most effective leaders, every day is New Year's Day.

I'm as guilty as the next person of finding the impending resetting of the calendar a cathartic cleansing, where the failures of the past year are suddenly washed away and replaced by the empty and unknown space filled with promise and time stretching out in front of us. There is something remarkably powerful and alluring about the chance to start-over, right wrongs and vow to do things right the next time around.

Resolutions start out as good intentions early in a new year and often end up as regrets later. At some point during the year, we cross a threshold where we mentally give up on the resolutions for now and resolve to succeed next year.

Full disclosure, I live in Chicago, where the saying "wait till next year" (Cubs) is slightly more commonplace than, "vote early and vote often." Waiting until next year is a part of the genetic make-up for anyone born north of Adams Street.

Real Time Resolutions Are Performance Fuel for Effective Leaders:

As a leader, you cannot afford to fall victim to the boom and bust cycle of annual resolutions. Rather, your challenge is a daily one, requiring you to manage your practices and habits in a program of perpetual self-improvement. Of course, identifying the right improvements requires you to have a real-time feedback system and the ability to keep your ego in check while as objectively as possible processing the daily evidence on your own performance.

While the simple act of even contemplating the need to improve requires a great degree of self-awareness and emotional intelligence on the part of the leader, remember, we are talking about effective leaders. Ineffective leaders are blind, deaf and dumb to these issues.

Eight Key Questions to Resolve About Your Own Leadership Practices:

1. How am I positively and negatively impacting the performance of my team members?

2. What are people telling me (directly and indirectly) about my performance?

3. Are people comfortable offering suggestions on how I can help?

4. How do people respond to me? Do they shrink or grow in my presence?

5. What is the quality of my various interactions? Are we tackling or skirting the tough issues?

6. Do people treat me with deference or respect?

7. Do my practices stimulate creativity or drive compliance?

8. Are there new ideas and suggestions for improvements flowing from the team?

Armed with insights and feedback, the effective leader strives to improve his/her performance daily, creating a kind of Leader's Muscle Memory where good habits become ingrained and second nature and bad habits are constantly exercised away.

Rather than annual resolutions to improve, the time for reflection is during the drive or plane trip home, at night before going to sleep or in the morning armed with that fresh promise of a new day...not dissimilar from the promise of the new year.

Effective leaders operate with a constant sense of renewal, driven by an intense desire to succeed and to help others succeed. While not every effective leader thinks in the exact language and terms of the questions above, they do think in terms of the same issues. What's working? What's not? What can I do better?

The Bottom-Line for Now:

The great news about being a leader is that you control the ability to do the right things every day. Every encounter provides the opportunity to improve. No more "wait until next year" for you. Your next year is right now and every minute thereafter. Resolve to use those minutes wisely and leave no regret in your leadership wake.

Section 6

Surviving the Tough Days

A number of years ago, two good friends of mine, Paul and Eric, were working hard to help turn-around a momentarily struggling software firm. As CFO and CEO respectively, they spent their days and early evenings working with nervous employees, extremely nervous bankers, grumpy board members, consultants of questionable repute, and importantly, some paying customers. This was a remote assignment for both of these gentlemen, so they rented a house in town to simplify living arrangements for the long days and weeks required to get the firm back on track. In addition to serving as a place to sleep, the house quickly became a remote meeting place for employees, and on occasion, the location of a late night jam session. Both Paul and Eric are remarkably talented musicians. (Paul is also a gifted storyteller, preferring long, involved jokes and storylines. Former colleagues indicate that Paul's stories would range in duration between twenty minutes and several hours.)

As this story goes, it was the end of a long and particularly challenging day, and the two happened across the movie, "The Memphis Belle," a story about the travails of a World War II bomber and crew. Rumor has it Eric and Paul were enhancing their creativity with generous helpings of Thompson's bourbon, and in a sudden moment of clarity, they observed a number of parallels between the challenges and obstacles encountered by the crew of the Memphis Belle, and their own turn-around situation. A legal pad was produced and they proceeded to scribble down a series of business maxims they immediately named, "The Business Rules of the Memphis Belle." Rule number 17 is the operative one here: "If the flak (anti-aircraft fire) is heavy, you're on target," and "No flak, no target."

Much like Paul's great stories, I just took the long way around to offering that if you are doing your job as a leader, the days will be noisy and probably filled with flak. And to make matters worse, you will frequently find yourself flying through thick fog, just hoping not to fly into something while working to get back home safely. Take heart, because as Paul and Eric describe, "No flak, no target." In case you find yourself without the Thompson's to help, try a few of the essays in this section and then get back at it. You've got a mission to complete.

Chapter 36

In the Face of Strong Headwinds, Learn to Tack

If you've ever sailed, you know that the only way to succeed against a headwind is to turn the bow of a boat through the wind and move in a zigzag pattern towards your ultimate destination. This maneuver is called tacking, and it is repeated frequently, requiring constant adjustments and careful monitoring of wind and sail angle to ensure forward progress without wasting precious time and energy.

The Best Leaders Tack Frequently Without Losing Sight of the Destination:

As leaders, we face dozens of moments every day where instinct tells us to turn straight into the wind and apply brute force to solve problems, resolve squabbles and keep people moving. Sometimes, our instinct is wrong.

Instead of offering a quick solution or mandating an end to squabbling, effective leaders adjust their course by engaging people, asking questions and helping individuals and groups discover for themselves how to resolve their issues. Much like catching the wind at precisely the right angle to fill the sails, effective leaders turn obstacles into energy, motion and progress.

John spent much of the first few years of his leadership career feeling like he was working hard without making forward progress. He did what he could to accommodate the people and personalities on his team, and he dutifully stepped into problems and provided quick solutions.

It took a new boss…someone who had learned the power of tacking against headwinds to show John that while he was managing his team on a daily basis, he wasn't truly leading. John quickly learned that accommodating people simply to keep the peace and stepping in to solve every major problem resulted in momentary compliance but little forward progress. As John changed his style, he marveled at what a difference it made for him and for his team members, as he helped them discover how to solve their own challenges.

Success Rarely Occurs in a Straight Line:

Too often, we develop our strategies and investment plans with the assumption that once implemented or released, life will be good, customers will line up to give us money and competitors will bow and back away, awestruck at our ability to outthink and out execute them. Ha!

The reality is that our projects flounder, our assumptions often crumble and the paper plans that were so precise and elegant in theory prove brittle and incomplete once they are put into play. Instead of an unfettered straight line to victory, success, if it comes at all, is only achieved by constant learning based on skillful navigation through crises and chaos.

Elizabeth was charged with responsibility for opening up a new market with a "game-changing" new product. Unfortunately, the only game that was changed was one that no customers were interested in playing, as measured by initial sales.

Instead of conceding defeat and giving up, Elizabeth and her team went back into the market to find out what had gone wrong. It turned out that their assumptions on the ease of implementation and the need for on-going support were way off. The team worked with customers to define a service offering to simplify the start-up phase, and they developed a dedicated support line to help quickly solve customer issues. As word spread on the value of the new offering and the great support from the firm, sales began to climb.

5 Ideas for Learning to Tack When Your Destination is Straight Into the Wind:

1. Defuse emotionally turbo-charged situations. Emotions create strong headwinds in the workplace. Learn to let people vent and then help them move into the mode of designing their way forward. This tacking in the face of emotional headwinds helps turn the negative energy into a positive force for forward progress.

2. Resist the urge to provide all of the answers. Remind everyone of the ultimate destination and then teach your team to develop, test and refine the solutions. Be quick to support learning and slow to criticize efforts.

3. Recognize and control your own tendency to fight the forces head-on. Organizational politics is best handled like fine china...delicately and only when necessary. I've observed otherwise capable people flame out after engaging in one too many extended firefights. Chances are, your political adversaries have something to teach you. Listen, learn and respond from a position of right and a position of strength.

4. Remember, your customers don't care about your goals, quotas or targets...they only care about their own priorities and problems. The best way to your destination is by adjusting your course to align with the one your customers want to be on.

5. Quit chasing competitors or you'll exhaust yourself getting nowhere. By the time you catch up to where they were, they'll be long gone. Set your own course..and perhaps they'll end up trying to chase you.

The Bottom-Line for Now:

We face all sorts of headwinds in our personal and professional lives. If you feel like you are constantly heading into the wind, it's probably time to adjust your course and put the wind to work for you. Just don't lose sight of your final destination.

Chapter 37

Eight Ideas for Remaining Personally Strong as a Leader

The paternal twins, Arrogance and Laziness, are experts at biding their time and waiting for an opening to slip into your leadership party. Constant vigilance is the only way to keep these destructive gatecrashers from moving in and taking up residence as permanent parts of your leadership style.

The twins, Arrogance and Laziness, look for small openings in your leadership defenses. Laziness knows that almost everyone reaches a point in time when they grow fatigued from their efforts. Great leaders appropriately question whether they are making a difference, wonder where they will find the fuel to keep going and even wonder what life would be like with no one to worry about on a daily basis. **It's at this point that Laziness sees an opening and offers an alluring set of suggestions:**

- *Don't work so hard. You've earned a rest. Just ease off a little.*
- *They'll figure it out on their own.*
- *You're not a career counselor.*

- *What's the point? You're fighting a no-win battle.*
- *I'm not playing politics here. I've already earned my stripes.*

Arrogance is never far behind, offering a similar but slightly more aggressive set of options:

- *Do it because I said so.*
- *I don't need your opinion to make this decision.*
- *I don't care what the facts say; we're going this way.*
- *Can't you see that I'm busy?*
- *I'm right, that's why they pay me.*

You are to be forgiven if you grow tired from time to time. It happens to the best of leaders and professionals. And lapsing into something that resembles arrogance is possible for most leaders…even the saintly ones. These are human issues, and only the leaders of myth and legend are immune to these failings. However, those that take their role seriously and strive to live it daily, employ a variety of approaches to avoid or minimize these lapses. They are aware of the allure Arrogance and Laziness and they work hard to keep them at bay.

8 Ideas for Remaining Strong as a Leader:

1. Move the body and it will take care of your mind. Exercise, a good diet, frequent walks around the office, a jaunt around the block at lunch or simply standing up and stretching all help keep the brain fresh, happy and focused on the rights issues in the right way. There's a ton of research that supports this, but the true test is in how good and fresh you feel when you do it. Personally, I like hiking a few flights of stairs…sometimes several times, just to clear the mind and gain the strength to tackle a tough problem.

2. Feed the mind. Take time to read (or listen to someone read) every day. Whether you are in the car, on the train, sitting in the airport lounge or contemplating watching the latest episode of your favorite show, choose to read something by someone that stimulates, challenges and encourages you to look at the world in a different way. A good goal…read something that challenges you and exposes you to new ideas for thirty minutes every day.

3. Feed the spirit. Your faith and/or your spirituality offer ample opportunities to refresh. This is a distinctly personal issue, but whether you take the time to pray in the fashion of your faith or consider your small place in the big picture as part of your view on the universe, adding this into your day can help remind you of how you've chosen to live your life personally and as a leader.

4. Create an early warning system. Find a trusted advisor…ideally a peer, who's comfortable and capable of telling you that you're acting like a moron. It's up to you to listen, and then take corrective action. And remember, your gut instinct will be denial.

5. Minimize the number of times you use the personal pronoun, "I" in conversations. Excessive use of this term is an indicator that Arrogance has set up shop. The key here is recognizing what is excessive versus normal and expected.

6. Talk less and ask more. In the same vein as the use of the term, "I," challenge yourself to talk less in meetings, ask more questions, and importantly, avoid criticizing answers. Just focusing on strengthening in these three areas will help you reinvigorate your leadership approach.

7. Do something truly humbling outside of work. This fits nicely in feeding the spirit, and will remind you of how good things are for you and how truly bad they can be given different circumstances.

8. If it fits your life stage, sign up to help coach your child's sports team. There's nothing like observing the exuberance and freedom of children playing a game for the fun of it, to remind you where you came from and who you are. One of my favorite moments as a parent was watching my young son and his good friend playing goalie and defender on their 4th grade soccer team. The action was on the other side of the field, and these two were having a great time picking dandelions and laughing. Pure and priceless!

The Bottom-Line for Now:

It's a great day to get over yourself! Now go pick some dandelions and then help someone do something great!

Chapter 38

Your Leadership Character is Forged in Defeat

"I firmly believe that any man's finest hour, his greatest fulfillment to all he holds dear, is the moment when he has worked his heart out in a good cause and lies exhausted, but victorious, on the field of battle."–Vince Lombardi

Everyone loves a winner. As a society, we like watching and reading about winners. We worship our sports heroes and we study and celebrate the great victories of history.

Hundreds of millions of people around the globe watch the Super Bowl every year, but only five or so can name the losers for the past three years. We remember the winners and we immediately relegate the losers to the trivia books.

Winning is great. It's often the culmination of years of hard work, a relentless focus on conditioning and on perfecting execution. What high school or college football coach hasn't hung a poster in the locker or training room with Vince Lombardi's inspirational quote listed at the opening of this essay?

It's easy to lose track of the reality that most victories are forged in the emotional blast furnace of prior losses. It's the losses and outright failures in life and business that either beat you down or fuel your competitive fires to work towards Lombardi's metaphorical field of victory.

Now don't get me wrong, I'm definitely not in favor of going out and seeking losses if you don't have to. However, unless you are one of the rare ones that leads a charmed existence, chances are that you will suffer setbacks, both large and small. Your response to those setbacks is the measure of your character.

You will be a part of projects that will flounder and fail. People you invest in will fail or worse yet, they will turn on you. Not every customer will buy from you, and competitors won't lie down and let you pass without a fight. You'll choose strategies that will turn out to be wrong, or, you'll choose good strategies but suffer from a failure to execute or motivate.

The life of a leader is filled with character building opportunities. Our scoreboards, performance measures and quarterlies tell part of the story, but victory as a leader takes place over a much longer period of time than we are accustomed to measuring.

Hey, I love great short-term numbers. I love the thrill of hitting and exceeding targets and the nice payday is good as well. But those victories are hollow compared to winning the real game. Your victory as a leader will be reported years from now, perhaps long after you've walked off the field. Take a glance back and see what you've left behind.

If you've left a trail of professionals and leaders in your wake, that are succeeding and successful and happily serving others, then you've won. Don't worry about the failures. They made you stronger, they taught you how to succeed and they fueled the fire that ultimately forged your leadership character.

Today's challenges might seem overwhelming. They're truly nothing more than a momentarily stumble or misstep on a long road. Take the time to face up to failure, reflect upon the lessons learned and then begin moving forward towards your next victory.

Regular readers of my blog know I cannot resist looking to history for inspiration. Lincoln faced defeat after defeat and a string of failed generals that left him truly the loneliest man in a divided America. He eventually got it right. Washington might just have the worst Win-Loss record in the annals of military generals. We all know the outcome.

Failure can beat you down and break you if you let it. The true leaders grimace, feel the burn in their bellies and then laugh and move forward.

The Bottom-Line for Now:

Laugh today and keep moving forward. There are lessons to be learned from stumbling while on the road to victory.

Chapter 39

It's Time for a Gut Check of
Your Intestinal Fortitude

Leading others is darned hard and often lonely work.
Do you have the "gut" for it?

Someone once asked me whether there was one quality above all others that stuck out as essential for success as a leader? Without hesitating, I responded, "intestinal fortitude."

Successfully leading others rates a difficulty factor on par with brain surgery, rocket science and throwing a no-hitter in baseball. And while I suspect that the brain surgeons, rocket scientists and professional pitchers may protest just a bit, consider the case for the extreme difficulty of leading and the need for intestinal fortitude:

Leading would be easy if it weren't for the people. We are complex, emotional creatures, all driven by our often unspoken intentions, dreams or battles. We're complex to guide, motivate, inspire and coach, and we don't easily place our trust in those that we reference as leaders.

For those keeping score, the days of frustration always outnumber the days of satisfaction. Accolades and hearty slaps on the back are uncommon responses to your best leadership efforts. In reality, the best moments of a leader are often celebrated in silence.

Ambiguity, uncertainty and change are on the menu daily. As a leader, you'll leave your comfort zone far behind, and you quickly discover that someone moves your cheese almost every day.

On the worst days, you'll stare in the mirror in the morning and be certain that you've finally reached your level of incompetence.

Back to intestinal fortitude (IF). IF is what kicks you out of bed every day, knocks down your demons of self-doubt, scoffs at ambiguity and gives you the confidence to serve, develop and guide others. IF helps you deal with ethical dilemmas, tough decisions and the sticky spots along the way. And finally, IF is what you draw upon to gain the courage and energy to persevere on what may often seem like a thankless task. It reminds you that this job has little to do with you and everything to do with the people around you.

Six Gut Check Questions on Your Intestinal Fortitude:

1. How much personal satisfaction do you gain from serving others? If your honest answer is, "not very much," then you need to reset on your leadership ambitions. If you truly do enjoy the ability to positively impact others through your role, recognize that you are running a marathon, not a sprint.

2. Do you miss the spotlight that sometimes comes with being a well-regarded individual contributor? Remember, the job you signed up for is almost never about you. Your success is measured in part by how many people other than yourself you can thrust into the spotlight.

3. Do you prefer to drive home every night feeling like you accomplished something? Hey, remember that crack in #1 above about marathons and sprints? This isn't like building a house or cutting the lawn. You may not see your accomplishments for years in some cases. Learn to measure success in terms of progress and development instead of tasks completed.

4. Miss the days when you were mostly in charge of your own schedule? I can't help you recapture those days, but I can offer some guidance to reassert control in the right areas. Build your calendar around developmental discussions, coaching sessions and feedback discussions and minimize the number of status and update meetings you attend. Remember, you're in a role to serve others. Instead of stressing over the time serving, cut some of the crap out of your calendar and you'll feel better about your days.

5. Hate making decisions that leave some people unhappy? Would you rather be on the receiving end of someone making these decisions for you? Probably not. Your decision-making autonomy is a measure of both your power and your success. People provide decision-making authority to those they trust, and by the nature of your existence in this role, someone has decided to trust you. This is a privilege, not a burden.

6. Uncomfortable taking the heat for the work of your team-members? Instead of stressing over being accountable for others, focus on doing what you can to help others achieve great results. And regardless of how great your team is, there will be times when you need to shield your team members from external pressures. These are truly remarkable opportunities to build credibility and strengthen everyone's view of you as a leader. Remember, everyone's watching your performance in these situations. And never forget the Coach's Rule: *if the team wins it's because of the team. If the team loses, it's because of the coach.*

The Bottom-Line for Now:

Leadership. It's not for the squeamish. From time-to-time your Intestinal Fortitude is all you have to help you get through the day. How strong is yours?

Chapter 40

Seven Suggestions for Cultivating
Your Crisis Leadership Skills

When faced with unexpected challenges, a good friend of mine intones a fitting old Yiddish quote, "Men Plan and God Laughs." Our modern incarnation of that is a less reverent but eminently understandable, "Stuff Happens!" Learning to cope with the unexpected deviation from your most carefully laid plans is an important part of growing up as a leader.

T he most challenging work and life experiences are the ones that shape and mold our character and help us earn the rare and valuable attribute of wisdom.

Of course, it's hard to sit back when the crap is hitting the proverbial fan and think, "Gee, I'm going to come out of this stronger and wiser." Instead of reflecting on your predicament, it's helpful to have your own approach to cope and act. There will be ample time for reflection down the road.

7 Suggestions for Cultivating Your Crisis Leadership Skills:

1. Early recognition of an emerging crisis is critical. Teach your team members to use their senses and sources to identify and report problems as early as possible. This is harder than it sounds and many otherwise smart leaders establish cultures that discourage early reporting without the whole picture being available. Don't shoot your messengers. Encourage them to look and listen for patterns or signs of problems and to be comfortable taking action to stomp out smoldering fires or to highlight approaching firestorms. Accurate, early recognition may save the day. It might even save your job.

2. Panic and confusion are powerful distractions. Eradicate them as quickly as possible. Train the people around you to quickly shift from shock and confusion to solution development. Establish processes for quickly and unemotionally assessing damage. Encourage rapid brainstorming for solution identification and get people working instead of preoccupying on the negative emotions. Words of warning: I've watched as teams and leaders squandered precious months attempting to determine whether a problem was real. Don't fall into this fatal time trap.

3. Know that the team mirrors your approach to the crisis. I mentioned shifting gears earlier. YOU need to find another performance and leadership gear that sets the tone and tenor for the team. If you flail, panic and show fear, your team's ability to accurately process and respond will melt away. A concerned and confident demeanor is critical.

4. It's time to trust others to do their jobs. You might have the title and earn the big bucks for being in charge, but now is not the time to assume that you have to think of everything. If you've cultivated, trained and empowered your team properly, it's time to trust them to execute their jobs. If you cannot trust them, you've got bigger leadership problems than the crisis at hand.

5. It's OK to issue essential orders in a crisis, but don't micromanage! While seemingly contradictory to my "trust" mandate above, I've observed leaders who failed to galvanize an effective response to a crisis by allowing people to spend too much time trying to figure out what to do next. This is a balancing act. Don't hesitate to issue orders on items critical to getting your team to the next step of managing the crisis. This is why you get paid the big bucks. Earn them.

6. Help your team members breakdown overwhelming tasks into discrete, manageable steps. Individuals and teams are easily paralyzed when the scale of a problem or a fix seems overwhelming. Emphasize discrete steps and focus efforts on what's out in front and fixable right now. The best way to eat an elephant is still one bite at a time.

7. Manage the environment. The effective crisis leader stays involved and aware of what's working and what's not. Encouragement, support, resources, help, decisions and knowing when to stay out of the way are all critical tasks and tools of the crisis leader.

The Bottom-Line for Now:

One of the worst mistakes that you can make as a leader is to assume that because you said, "Make it so," your plans will magically unfold without so much as a hiccup. Whether you subscribe to the belief that "Stuff Happens," or "Man Plans and God Laughs," you are well served to recognize that a large part of your role is helping others navigate problems.

Develop an approach that allows you to leverage these great opportunities to teach, to test and to cultivate leadership skills in others. You will learn a great deal about yourself and your team members in the process.

Chapter 41

Seven Odd Ideas to Help You Get Unstuck

While some argue that the natural order of life is towards entropy (a gradual decline into disorder), I would argue that the natural tendency of most humans is towards a kind of comfortable sameness and consistency in their daily lives. Beware of creeping comfort. It saps energy, stifles innovation and makes you part of the problem, not the solution.

The pursuit of opportunity requires more energy than the slow descent into routine. It is most definitely easier to not change. There is comfort in routine. It feels good, like the hot shower and the well-worn sweats that you put on after a long day at work.

We like to see familiar surroundings and familiar faces. Consider a situation as trivial as your health club and your workout routine. There's comfort in seeing the same, often nameless people at 5:30 a.m. We belong, we are one of them, and everything is in balance when we assume our place with this familiar group. Shift your workout to a mid-day routine, and the entire feel of the place changes, although the facilities and equipment are the same. It's different and slightly discomforting.

While comfortable, routine is the enemy of growth, progress and innovation. Routine is carried out in muscle memory. Spend too much time doing the same things the same way and existence becomes one of pre-programmed decisions and choices that carve deep mental ruts in our minds that make change all the more difficult.

Routine is the enemy of growth. The false comfort of sameness masks a slow decline and ultimately decay. High performance individuals in all areas of life, from leaders to athletes to great individual contributors work hard every day to fight the gravitational pull of getting stuck in the proverbial rut. High performance teams and organizations find their comfort not in sameness or routine, but in embracing the ambiguity of the world and the constancy of change and the constant need to change.

The best leaders I've known, go out of their way to push themselves and their teams to constantly do things in different ways to keep their senses sharp, their individual and collective minds expanding and their ideas fresh. They work hard at getting and staying unstuck!

Seven Ideas to Help Leaders and Teams Get Unstuck:

1. Fight the tyranny of the Outlook calendar and recurring meetings. There are few things worth talking about over and over again, and yet many in organizations perceive that they are doing their jobs by scheduling and conducting these self-aggrandizing events. Fight the tyranny of others ruling your calendar!

2. Rotate leadership. More and more organizations are adopting an IDEO-inspired approach of choosing leaders for initiatives not based on seniority or level, but based on the group's assessment of who the right leader is to help the team succeed with the initiative at hand. Simple sounding…and in some organizations, heresy, but this is a true opportunity to innovate in management and more importantly, to ensure that every new initiative benefits from a fresh way of looking at things.

3. Break the back of bad-habit brainstorming! As odd as it sounds, I've observed a "sameness" and routine to brainstorming that is actually counter to the intended creative idea generating intent of the activity. Groups come together and rehash the same ideas that they didn't adopt in the last round. There's no edge, no excitement and nothing new as an outcome. Try introducing anonymity into the process (variations of the Delphi technique); add outsiders/newcomers to the group and mix up methods for post-brainstorming idea selection.

4. From time to time, do something completely off-task with your group. One manager creates vexing cases (business problems, people issues, strategy issues) that are different from but analogous to her work situation and facilitates the group through analysis and solution development. Just getting people to think about other problems in other fictional settings is helpful in creating new pathways for problems in the current setting.

5. Introduce your team to the management innovators and great leaders of today and yesterday. Another manager regularly exposes his team to other leaders, cultures and approaches leveraging the massive volume of content available on YouTube and increasingly at places like Harvard and Stanford. I do this in my management classes as well and long after the textbook and PowerPoint content is forgotten, people remember meeting (virtually) Jim Collins, Meg Whitman, Tony Hsieh, John Chambers, Guy Kawasaki, Eric Schmidt, Jack Welch, Jim Goodnight, Herb Kelleher and many other current and historic management innovators.

6. Play a game. One of my favorite activities to run is the Dollar Bill Auction, which is guaranteed to both be fun and teach everyone about the realities and dangers of escalation of commitment. (Search on the phrase and you will find ample references.)

One of my favorite professionals, Kay Wais, at Successful Projects, LLC is creating games for aspiring Project Managers, and has recently introduced a well-received Project Risk board game. I love the idea of introducing different ways of learning about important topics, and the game approach is fun and educational at the same time.

7. Change your personal routine. I recall observing a change in routine in one of my senior managers. He had noticeably changed his style of dress. He was arriving at work at a different time (earlier) and even parking on the other side of the building. When I inquired about the changes, his response was something to the effect of, "I'm pushing my team to mix things up in an effort to break out of our sales slump and it's helping me to think differently by changing up my old routines." Sales improved significantly the next quarter.

The Bottom-Line for Now:

Take comfort in being uncomfortable about being comfortable. If you followed that, you get my point in this essay. We talk endlessly about the accelerating pace of change in our world and we see it in play daily. And then many of us go back to our usual routine. It's time for you to recognize the need for change in yourself, and as a leader, for you to find ways to stimulate new thinking, promote different approaches and make the existence of change part of the excitement of working in this world.

Chapter 42
Learning to Ask for Help

Contrary to what you might think, you're not required to know all of the answers. However, you are required to know how to figure things out. The great leaders of history and all effective leaders in business have advisors and so should you. Whether you are asking your boss, your team members or a trusted colleague, developing an approach and developing comfort asking for help is an important skill.

I've not met a human being that doesn't need help from time to time, and this goes double for anyone in a leadership role. Leadership is frequently lonely and those who take their role seriously often face decisions surrounded by ambiguity and risk.

The pressure to "figure it out" is tremendous, partially imposed by our fast moving and politically charged working environments, and partially imposed by our own sense that to show we need help is to show weakness. I've known otherwise good leaders that derailed because they ended up in situations where Solomon himself would have sought advice, yet personal and perceived environmental pressures kept them from reaching out to others.

Some of the fears and pressures are real. There's no doubt in my mind that there is a boundary line that can be crossed where a person goes from legitimately needing help to just plain needy. Your challenge is to learn to use "Help" as a tool and to honor that boundary.

Seven Ideas for Elegantly and Professionally Asking for Help:

1. Frame the situation. Your success in gaining help is directly related to how clearly you can describe the dilemma. Spend time thinking through the "frame" of the problem. Organize the information in your mind and on paper in a way that will quickly provide context for others.

2. Plan your message. What's clear in your mind may sound fairly random and confusing to someone else unless you organize your message. Develop a simple message map to guide your communication. Place the core message or issue at the center of the map, and then surround your core message with no more than four major supporting points. While there are likely dozens of points, work hard to thrift your message down to the key issues. Of course, be prepared with data, facts, expert opinions and whatever else you require to support your points.

3. Don't forget the risks. Identify the risks of not addressing the situation to show that you have thought through the implications to the team, the individual and to your firm. However, be careful not to over-state or over-dramatize the risks or the next time you won't be taken seriously. Highlight the most salient issues and implications as part of your narrative.

4. Never ask for help naked. Now that I have your attention, what I mean to say is: form and frame your key questions for help ahead of time. If you deliver your narrative and then just stop or throw out the, "I'm just not certain what to do," statement, you are passing the problem over to someone else, and they will resist and even resent this move on your part. After describing your core issue, the key supporting points and risks, suggest a finite number of best alternatives and break down the pros and cons of each. Ask for input, ask what other questions jump to mind, ask about prior experiences, and don't be afraid to offer your own favored solution and ask for feedback.

5. Never ask, "What do you think I should do?" This is another question that leaves you exposed and attempts to shift your burden to someone else.

Remember, it's your job to tell us what you think you should do and the other person's job to help you think through your logic. Most managers are OK offering help if you approach them properly. Take the time to study and learn your manager's preferences when it comes to guiding others. Some enjoy getting into the details and others want the big picture along with your assessment of the risks and your recommendations. Provide too much detail to the latter manager or jump too far ahead of the manager that feels good helping you work through the issues, and you've misfired and missed a good opportunity to strengthen your relationship with your boss.

6. Tap into your peer network. Everyone should invest time cultivating a group of individuals who will provide unvarnished feedback and generally serve as an informal board of advisors. These are the people who will challenge you to improve and advance. They will give you tough love when you need it and help you avoid critical decision-making traps. While it takes effort to develop a quality network, the dividends are potentially huge.

7. Tap into your team. While this may seem counter-intuitive and it certainly flies in the face of the mistaken self-image of the all-knowing boss, your team members probably have a collectively clear view of the problem and potential solutions. And, the act of asking and then listening to your team members will do wonders for your credibility.

The Bottom-Line for Now:

We all need help from time to time and it's both wise and acceptable to seek it out in the proper fashion. Asking for help is not an admission of weakness, it's an attempt to tap into the strengths of others. Just remember that you own the heavy lifting required to reach the point where others will gladly shoulder a bit of the burden.

Chapter 43

The Artful and Effective Workplace Apology

"The secret to my success as a leader in my business has been my ability to offer a well-timed and heartfelt apology after mucking things up."

The gentleman who offered up this "secret to success" certainly used this tool wisely, judging by the growth of his business over the years and the loyalty and respect I hear in the words of his employees.

The apology is an often over-looked and widely misunderstood tool for keeping smoldering bridges from burning out of control and for repairing relationships that were dented somewhere in the chaos of the day. It's also a tool easily misused by people uncomfortable in their roles and seeking to buy compliance by apologizing their way forward.

For Some Leaders, It's Hard to Form the Words:

Some leaders find it difficult to apologize for their transgressions, in part, due to the fear of being perceived as weak, when just the opposite is true. It's difficult to own up to our mistakes and awkward to get in front of those who were adversely impacted and say, *"I was wrong and I apologize."*

Others find it difficult to apologize due to a mistaken belief that their title buys them the equivalent of a human relations "Get Out of Jail Free" card. Newsflash: your title doesn't entitle you to be a jerk.

Ample Ammunition for Apologies:

Stuff happens in the course of daily business. Crises erupt, emotions fly and it's all too easy for people to misstep and misspeak in the heat of the moment. A poorly stated piece of feedback, an off-handed comment, failure to provide your full attention when someone truly needed it, or a broken or forgotten commitment are all apology-worthy transgressions.

The Power of a Well-Placed and Heartfelt Apology:

- **You display your authenticity as a human being.** People respond better to authentic leaders than those who work too hard to mask their frailties and flaws.

- **You exercise your social intelligence skills.** Ultimately, your ability to read and engage effectively with people will determine your success. It's important to learn how to recognize when you've sent someone down the wrong path with your poor behavior.

- **You gain some street credibility for making the effort.** While you don't automatically reset credibility lost through your apology-worthy behavior, you can buy another chance to build trust.

- **Your honesty sets a healthy tone in the workplace.** People make mistakes and instead of sweeping them under the carpet, you are modeling good behavior for everyone to follow.

5 Tips for Constructing an Appropriate, Effective Apology:

A Well-Constructed Apology is:

1. Timely-As close to the transgression as possible, please.

2. Specific-By describing what you did wrong and why it was wrong, you are showing your command of yourself and your awareness of the impact you have on people and on the workplace.

3. Behavioral-Try: Here's what I intended and why…here's what I did…and I understand that my approach failed to communicate what I intended.

4. Genuine-Say what you mean and mean what you say.

5. Brief-No one wants you to draw it out. Don't excuse it, don't make excuses for your behavior and don't try and describe the twenty things that happened that day that added up to your bad moment.

5 Common Apology Mistakes to Avoid:

1. Apologizing as a tactic to assert your agenda. "Hey, I'm sorry to ask you to this, but… ." Don't be sorry for asking, and no "buts" please.

2. Saying: "I'll make it up to you." You cannot buy your way out of a mistake. The apology is enough.

3. Not apologizing when you've mucked up. Get over yourself and get on with it.

4. Waiting too long. If something you did merits an apology, chances are you irked or upset someone in the process. The longer this festers, the greater the adverse impact on your relationship with the individual or team.

5. Bringing it up repeatedly. Once is enough if you do it right. No need to carry around endless guilt and no need to open old wounds. Let go and move forward.

The Bottom-Line for Now:

Unless your membership card to the human race was repealed, you will make mistakes that merit apologies. Effective leaders manage themselves and their mistakes with grace and professionalism, and as uncomfortable as it may be, apologizing is occasionally on the menu. Please make it digestible for all parties involved.

Chapter 44

Don't Expect Easy-My Top 15 Suggestions for Coping as a Professional

"Easy" is not a term that should be on your mind, except when it comes to improving the experience for your customers. Outside of making life easier for your customers, there are few circumstances where "easy" shows up or where you are justified in expecting things to go that way.

If you're at the early stage of your career, the transition from school to job is an interesting one filled with learning experiences and adjustments. Things probably aren't as "easy" as they once seemed. And of course, if you've been around the block a few times, you've long since concluded that "easy" is rare indeed.

Things That Are Most Definitely Not Easy in Business:

- Working for a difficult boss.

- Becoming a boss.

- Becoming a good boss.

- Finding great people.

- Hiring the right people.
- Undoing the process of hiring the wrong people.
- Competing in the market.
- Competing internally.
- Leading without authority.
- Creating a new strategy.
- Implementing a new strategy.
- Getting others to follow you.
- Following others.
- Making decisions.
- Making mistakes.
- Learning from mistakes.
- Taking risks, knowing that they might be mistakes.
- Developing as a senior contributor.
- Switching jobs.
- Switching careers.
- Continuing your education.
- Reinventing yourself.
- Balancing life and work.

My Top 15 Suggestions for Coping with the Tough Stuff:

I've known a few people that seemed to have a free pass through life's difficulties, but for the rest of us, here are my suggestions and words of encouragement:

1. Attitude is everything. Make certain that yours stays positive about the challenges in front of you.

2. There is no substitute for hard work. Keep pushing the rock up the hill.

3. Success is in the details. Don't be a 70-percenter. Learn to finish.

4. It's all about learning. Mistakes are your best teachers. Just don't make the same mistakes twice.

5. As my former boss would say, "Man plans and God laughs." Interpret that to mean that things mostly don't go as you expect them to.

6. Hope is a crappy strategy. See also the note on hard work.

7. You'll make mistakes. Don't wallow for more than a few minutes. Take your medicine, make a mental note to learn something, and then shrug your shoulders and move on to your next challenge.

8. There are no guarantees. *Enough said.*

9. There are no shortcuts. You'll have to work for everything you get. Get over it.

10. "Fear is the mind-killer." I love this quote from Frank Herbert. Don't let fear rule your life.

11. Measure-twice and cut once. An extra emphasis on quality will serve you well.

12. Compensation is nice, but there's more to life than money. Ultimately, enough is enough.

13. It's a hollow goal to just chase the money.

14. The joy is in the journey, not the destination.

15. Touch people in the right way during your journey. You go through this once. Make it count.

The Bottom-Line for Now:

No one owes you "easy." Get over it and get on with it. And don't forget to try and make it just a bit easier for those following behind you. It's the least you can do.

Section 7

Building and Leading High Performance Teams

I have a hard time resisting the urge to poll audiences in workshops, keynotes and other meetings on various topics about their leadership and work experiences. It's ready-made, down and dirty market research, and while it wouldn't pass muster with a professional journal, it most definitely can give us the temperature on some particularly important topics.

One of my frequent areas of inquiry focuses on people's experiences on high performance teams. More specifically, I am always interested in whether people believe they've been a part of a team that they are comfortable describing as high performance. Of course, there are always the nitpickers in the audience who make us define high performance before casting their votes. Once we get mundane things like definitions out of the way, the results are consistent from group to group. Less than fifty-percent of professionals in these settings indicate that they've ever been part of something they would describe as "high performance." That's disturbing and just a bit depressing.

Given the project-centricity of our world and the realities of distributed, cross-cultural work teams, it's safe to say that you must develop your skills at leading and participating on project teams. Whether you are serving as a formal or informal leader, it's in your best interest to cultivate team experiences that are highly productive and somewhat enjoyable. Of course, this would be easy if it weren't for the people.

This section is intended to whet your appetite for developing, leading and participating on high performance teams. Here's hoping you and yours can help raise the batting average a bit higher. I look forward to reporting back on very different results from my polling activities in a few years!

Chapter 45

Want a Dream Team? Give a Visionary a Voice

Who's the Visionary on your team? Hint: chances are it's not the leader. Contrary to popular myth, "being a visionary" is neither a prerequisite for leading, nor is it bestowed upon the chosen few as they ascend to their lofty perches above us.

Many Visionaries labor in relative obscurity, often ignored or worse yet, mocked, because of their unique way of looking at the world and the issues in front of them.

If you are leading and are interested in building or creating something more than an efficient machine with your team, you are well served to seek out and cultivate those individuals who are capable of seeing patterns and pictures in the environment that the rest of us miss.

You know these people. They are the ones that sit quietly in meetings while the inane debates rage over how to solve grossly tactical issues and they will occasionally look up and say, "Why don't we?" or, "What if we did it this way?" After a few moments of silence, someone will usually chime up and say, "Yeah, Mary has a point, what if we... ?" With a simple comment or observation, the entire direction of the conversation shifts...often for the better.

Consider this Most Famous of Conversations:

Lucy Van Pelt: "Aren't the clouds beautiful? They look like big balls of cotton. I could just lie here all day and watch them drift by. If you use your imagination, you can see lots of things in the cloud's formations. What do you think you see, Linus?"

Linus Van Pelt: "Well, those clouds up there look to me look like the map of the British Honduras on the Caribbean."
[*points up*]

Linus Van Pelt: "That cloud up there looks a little like the profile of Thomas Eakins, the famous painter and sculptor. And that group of clouds over there..."
[*points*]

Linus Van Pelt: "...gives me the impression of the Stoning of Stephen. I can see the Apostle Paul standing there to one side."

Lucy Van Pelt: "Uh huh. That's very good. What do you see in the clouds, Charlie Brown?"

Charlie Brown: "Well... I was going to say I saw a ducky and a horsie, but I changed my mind."
(*from the site: The Internet Movie Database-memorable quotes from the movie, A Boy Named Charlie Brown.*)

The Visionary in this situation is of course the blanket-toting Linus...the odd little kid who is operating on a different level than the rest of the gang. When it comes to cloud gazing, I suspect that I am more like Charlie Brown in that exchange!

One of my favorite visionaries reads my blog regularly. (I suspect he knows who he is, although I doubt anyone ever offered him the label.) This technologist propelled an entire organization on his ideas. While his "visions" were not universally admired by peers or instantly accepted, the fact was and is that his ideas solve technology conundrums for customers in remarkable ways. Note: visionaries often have detractors.

Sometimes you need to look hard to find the Visionary on your team. In my own experience, they are not the classic "A" players that work circles around the rest of the team. They aren't the loudest...in fact quite the opposite. They don't tend to gravitate to the limelight.

Five Tips for Cultivating the Visionaries on Your Team:

1. Once you uncover someone that has more to offer than the transactional demands of the job, cultivate a relationship with the individual. Take the time to carve out one-on-one time and to discuss vexing issues.

2. Don't thrust the Visionary into the spotlight if he/she is uncomfortable with the visibility.

3. Place Visionaries on project teams where the challenges require new ways of doing things.

4. Align Visionaries with Doers. My best teams have blended both in the right proportion to ensure both innovation and execution.

5. And fair warning: be careful to not bestow a special label on the individual or you risk alienating him or her further and damaging your own credibility. This isn't an issue of playing favorites, it's one of extracting the often quiet and potentially valuable voice on your team.

The Bottom-Line for Now:

I'll end where I started. Want a dream team? Give a Visionary a voice.

Chapter 46
Develop a Big Picture View or
Risk Becoming a Carp

Far too many leaders that I work with lack awareness of the broader forces swirl-
ing around their firms, their customers and those shape-shifting clusters that we
describe as industries. Given the hurricane like market and societal forces buffet-
ing our globe today, a strategy of boarding up the windows and hunkering down
is tantamount to committing corporate suicide.

I cannot rationalize why some firms lack the systems and cultural elements that encourage environmental scanning, assessment and action formulation, but I can empathize just a bit. The world is a complex place and increasingly, planning and managing businesses for value creation has become a "Wicked Problem" where the volume of con-tradictory and conflicting information is overwhelming. Ignoring this complexity and focusing on controllable issues and digestible problems is an understandable human response. In many cases, taking an Occam's Razor approach (the simplest solution is usually the best solution) is much better than falling victim to the malady of complexity induced organiza-tional paralysis. However, in cases where a firm marches along oblivi-ous and/or unresponsive to the swirling forces constantly reshaping the world it is a wholesale failure of leadership.

There are no miracle cures or silver bullets for making sense out of the chaos, other than the hard work of paying attention, assessing and either reacting or pro-acting as the occasion merits. Building a learning culture is essential to survival, not just success. For real-time examples of firms that don't and did not get it, pick up any newspaper. And while the smaller firms in our economy don't grab the headlines, the failures and the failing are epidemic here as well. At least part of this epidemic stems from a failure of top leaders to comprehend the destructive power of the broader market forces until right after their firms have been flattened.

How the Lowly Carp Fits Into this Story:

The physicist and author, Dr. Michio Kaku uses the following personal anecdote to challenge people to think beyond the confines of their current four dimensions into the possibilities of a much more complex and much larger universe:

"When I was a child, I used to visit the Japanese Tea Garden in San Francisco. I would spend hours fascinated by the carp, who lived in a very shallow pond just inches beneath the lily pads, just beneath my fingers, totally oblivious to the universe above them. I would ask myself a question only a child could ask: what would it be like to be a carp? What a strange world it would be! I imagined that the pond would be an entire universe, one that is two-dimensional in space. The carp would only be able to swim forwards and backwards, and left and right. But I imagined that the concept of "up" beyond the lily pads, would be totally alien to them. Any carp scientist daring to talk about "hyperspace", i.e. the third dimension "above" the pond, would immediately be labeled a crank. Today, many physicists believe that we are the carp swimming in our tiny pond, blissfully unaware of invisible, unseen universes hovering just above us in hyperspace. We spend our life in three spatial dimensions, confident that what we can see with our telescopes is all there is, ignorant of the possibility of 10 dimensional hyperspace. While fascinated by the opportunities and possibilities of 10-dimensional hyperspace, the comparison in this post is to those that operate in the confines of their firms and traditional industry boundaries, without sticking their heads out

of the pond to observe the broader world and the impact that it is having on their personal pond."

Nine Suggestions for Not Becoming A Carp-Or, How to Improve Your Team's External Awareness and Chances of Survival:

1. Establish the audacious goal of creating a cultural evolution to increase your team's/firm's external awareness AND ability to act. Many of the following points support this goal.

2. Remind people regularly that it is their job to monitor and report on customers and competitors. Reinforce the "tell" by paying attention to what they have to say.

3. Create forums to discuss the external world and ensure that these forums don't succumb to the powerful gravitational pull of internal stuff.

4. Challenge business units and leaders to define "learning" strategies. Challenge IT to create systems that enable collection, translation and dissemination.

5. Ask and require answers to the questions: "What does this mean for us? Our customers? Our future?"

6. Connect external factors and internal hypotheses to improvement and innovation actions and measure the results of these efforts.

7. Run strategy reviews with an emphasis on connecting what's happening externally to how resources are being used/invested internally. If there is no connection, blow up the project.

8. Recognize the need to use the tools of management...especially structure as a means to create value out of changing forces. While your current processes and culture might not support responding to change by building the product that will cannibalize your business, a dedicated project team, a spin-out or an acquired firm might enjoy a higher probability of success. Don't hesitate to make bold moves with teams and structures to achieve your objectives.

9. Seek out varied perspectives. Constantly. Remember, asking another carp in the pond about the world outside the pond will only get you another perspective from the pond.

The Bottom-Line for Now:

This topic invariably invites debate and a fair amount of criticism, especially from top leaders who feel that my observations are an indictment of their efforts. And while I am most definitely offering criticism, my primary purpose is to encourage you as a leader to live up to your billing as a sentient being. While a carp may perceive the outcome of an environmental change, you and your team members are capable of assessing and taking action to survive and ideally prosper. Vow not to become a carp this year or any year.

Chapter 47

Six Ideas to Improve Team Performance

If your organization is like most, you're leaving money on the table in terms of team productivity and performance. Social and interpersonal factors, motivation issues, lack of group cohesion and the general up-front churn that teams display as they form, are just a few of the areas where you can pick up immediate productivity improvements with a little bit of smart leadership.

W e're all working on teams, with teams, for teams or, we're in the unenviable role of leading a team or two. If managing wasn't tough enough, now we're responsible for pulling together a group of already over-worked and over-stressed individuals and shaping them into a lean, mean project execution machine. And for your next trick, you'll make pigs sprout wings and fly around the office.

The formal practice of project management has grown tremendously over the past decade. The PMP (Project Management Professional) certification is a popular and hard-earned designation and more organizations than ever are adopting program management offices and project portfolio management practices to go along with the increase in the number of PMPs on staff. However, the gross majority of group, team or committee activities still fly below the radar of formal project management leadership and executive sponsorship. These are typically manager-led initiatives or cross-functional groups coming together to tackle a problem, and for at least one soul, he or she gets the opportunity to practice herding cats.

Six Ideas to Improve Team Performance Today:

1. First, control your urge to put a team on every problem that comes along. Use groups sparingly. Carefully assess whether a group effort truly stands the best chance of success. There are many situations where the right individual can work with stakeholders and across functions and accomplish the goals or solve the problem more efficiently and effectively than a team.

2. If you must establish a team, ensure that the goals are clear and compelling. Unclear goals promote "churn and flail" and mundane tasks drive lackadaisical performance. As the responsible organizational leader (not necessarily the work team leader), you must ensure that the goal of the initiative is crystal clear and linked to a key business imperative. Vague goals and unclear context are productivity and morale killers.

3. Rethink your approach to choosing team leaders. Instead of seniority or rank, work-team leadership must be based on a single criterion: "Who is the person best suited to help us succeed with the task at hand?" Depending upon the nature of the task, an individual with good facilitation skills, or a person that works well across functions might be better suited than a functional manager or the most senior person on the group. Just because you are the responsible person (sponsor), doesn't mean that you have to lead the day-to-day work efforts. Let the leader emerge or, have the team choose the leader.

4. Define the group's values up-front. Don't make a career out of this, but definitely don't skip describing and memorializing the required group behaviors for discussion, debate, attendance, participation and work-completion. If the values are clear, and accountabilities spelled-out in the opening phase, there's little maneuvering room for those attempting to wiggle-off the hook and get out of work.

5. Remember, simple assignments save time. Every meeting must have a note-taker (scribe), a timekeeper and a traffic cop. The traffic cop enforces the rules in play (e.g. brainstorming) and helps the team remain focused.

6. Always assign a coach. If the group is expected to work together for more than a few days, it is helpful to ask for an objective 3rd party to assess team processes and interpersonal dynamics. You don't need to spend money to bring in an outside resource with a fancy certification. One organization used representatives from HR (a great way to help get this group engaged with the business of business) and another identified a coaching role and rotated the responsibility between individuals. The coach is not part of the working team, but rather an occasional and objective observer that reports back to the designated team leader on group dynamics and group processes.

The Bottom-Line for Now:

We are well served to identify continuous improvement opportunities for our collaborative endeavors. I've watched great process companies with legions of people wearing colored belts forget about some of the simple suggestions above that can save money and time, spur performance and add to task enjoyment and morale. Today is a great day to help your teams and groups boost their performance!

Chapter 48

Team Conflict? As Long As
It's Not Personal, Run With It

I'm leery of happy teams. Don't get me wrong. I like positive experiences and working with happy people, however, in my experience, the happy teams are the ones that produce mediocre results or, they don't produce at all.

Give me a group of people that show up to battle on the issues versus the team that strives for peace and harmony, any day.

Just as "being liked" isn't required to be effective as a leader, neither is maintaining peace and harmony on the team required for success. What is required is the ability to push the envelope on creativity, talk openly and freely about problems and shortcomings, and to cry foul when someone violates the group's norms for performance, behavior and accountability. For many people, conflict in the team environment feels wrong. It's uncomfortable. Conflict breeds personal stress and group tension, and sometimes creates a hue and cry for "getting along." While an aversion to conflict is understandable if it is personal in nature, task and process conflict are important factors in propelling high-performance teams forward.

Five Reasons a Dose of Conflict Might Be Healthy For Your Team:

1. Elephants aren't allowed to hide in the room. The big issues and tough topics are uncovered quickly and dispatched without worrying about personal interests and political boundaries.

2. Social loafing is squashed. Hanging out and working at less than full tilt becomes painfully obvious in environments where the group is challenging itself to move together through the jungle. People pull their weight or they are left behind.

3. Decisions are held to a higher standard. While the potential pitfalls of group decision-making are well known, teams that challenge themselves and each other in pursuit of achievement tend to have higher standards for the quality of their decisions. Instead of a rush-to-decide or a drive-to-consensus culture found on more collegial teams, task-focused groups search for answers that pass the filters for both quality and speed. In my experience, they challenge assumptions, seek the right data and assess risks and implications much more effectively than the "let's all get along" teams.

4. Leadership skills are challenged and strengthened. High task conflict teams are leadership laboratories. One of the "elephants in the room" of my argument here is that leading these teams is not for the faint of heart. Team leaders must learn to manage the flow and energy of the conflict to ensure that it doesn't move into personal territory. They also need to be adept at helping maneuver the team from the heat of robust dialogue to a decision and implementation. These are clearly non-trivial leadership challenges and remarkable learning opportunities for all involved.

5. Standards for performance are enhanced. Participants refuse to settle for anything other than success, and success is often defined as either exceeding or obliterating targets or, innovating in some meaningful fashion. Task conflict pushes people higher and harder. Along the way, these high performance teams raise the bar for everyone in the organization.

The Bottom-Line for Now:

I suspect that I'm skating on thin-ice according to the number of people that have shared with me that they find conflict distressing and destructive. Keep in mind that my context is task or process conflict, and not anything personal in nature. It takes an emotionally intelligent group to pull this off and not let good and tough discussions over the right issues reduce to squabbling and paralysis. It's hard work to find and foster this type of a team and environment. But since when isn't high performance the outcome of hard work?

Chapter 49

Teach Your Team to Make Better Decisions

If you were to embark upon a rugged and lonely journey to the top of the mountain to ask for enlightenment from the Oracle of Management, I suspect that you would be left with the words "decision-making" to ponder on your long walk back to civilization. And while that might not sound much like enlightenment, remember that Oracles by their nature offer only vague but profound observations to stimulate learning.

In spite of the lack of a concrete answer from this journey, I'll throw in my two-cents worth that decision-making is in fact the essence of management. It's also darned hard to do, difficult to teach and challenging to get right more often than not.

As humans, we make tens of thousands of decisions ranging from the mundane to the profound. Decisions open up new paths, close off old ones and usher in an entirely new series of issues and decisions that ultimately affect us in so many ways that it is hard to fathom.

History can be explained in hindsight as a series of critical decisions that ultimately determined the fate of civilizations, empires, nations and tribes.

Think about your own professional experience. If you've spent any significant amount of time in the workplace, you can certainly look in the rear view mirror and see decision-points that impacted the fate of teams,

197

companies, or tasks. Projects hinge on decision-making effectiveness, as do new product launches and business strategies.

As a newly hired, early-career professional, I recall watching and listening as a firm's market leading position was sacrificed on the altar of ego and ignorance with a single utterance from an executive. "We're not going to compete at the low end of the market." Within two years, the marketplace was the low-end. Ironically and sadly, most of us in the room suspected that the decision was bad at the time. There were some polite objections, but no one was strong enough (at the time) to challenge the executive's decision.

Alternatively, I've participated in long and tough discussions and decision-making processes with teams that ultimately translated into good and great outcomes on both small and large scales. In hindsight, the decisions seem so clear and obvious, but in real-time, they were tense, ambiguous and even frightening.

Talent-related decisions are some of the most common and painful. Anyone who has hired a significant number of people has made one or more mistakes. What was it about your own decision-making process that failed you or that obfuscated your ability to assess the individual properly? It's hard to say, but chances are you've learned from that mistake and refined your process.

While machines can be taught to make decisions based on rules and data, humans have the advantage and disadvantage of being human. There are many complex factors at play in our decision-making processes. Our personalities, our personal experiences sets, our biases and many complicated environmental and risk and reward issues all combine to make effective decision-making a complex task.

On the other-hand, we're paid to make decisions and we're responsible for helping our groups and teams do this effectively more often than not. What's a leader to do?

The Bad News-There Are No Decision-Making Silver Bullets:

My review of much of the management literature on decision-making showcases a great deal of fascinating discussion without a lot of substantive guidance. Yep, we're pretty much on our own to wander blindfolded through the decision-making woods. As I look back on my own career (yep, there's that experience bias) as well as my observations of many, many teams and leaders, I've formed an informal and I'm sure imperfect, but hopefully, helpful list of tools to guide managers on strengthening their decision-making effectiveness and that of their teams.

Eleven Remarkably Helpful Ideas on Improving Personal and Team Decision Making:

1. People need context to make decisions. The best context in a firm starts with a galvanizing vision and is strengthened with a clear strategy and highly interconnected goals. If you've worked in firms with and without this clarity, you've lived and know the difference. The absence of vision, strategy and clear, meaningful goals equates to complete lack of context for any decisions. They are all good and bad and there is no way to discriminate. Fix this!

2. If your organization fails on point number one, YOU OWN fixing this at the team or group level. Quit complaining about the lack of guidance and define the playing field and goals for your team. Yes, this puts accountability on you and requires you to turn ambiguity into something concrete. Get over it and get on with it.

3. You set the pace for decision-making on your team. Your decision-making style infects and impacts everyone around positively or negatively. Ponder too long and the result is paralysis. React too quickly and you increase risk and the likelihood of team whiplash by finding that you have to quickly reverse decisions as additional clarity is gained. You must deliberately develop a style that balances the need for clarity with the reality that much of business is steeped in ambiguity.

4. Beware the evil paternal twins of groupthink and group polarization. Know your enemies and keep them visible and teach your teams how to keep them at bay.

5. Create diversity where there is none. Beware the potential for damage from hiring too many like-minded professionals on your team. They may be great professionals, but in group settings, their lack of diversity is a problem. Draw in people with varying perspectives and backgrounds to help challenge conventional thinking.

6. Keep the Devil's Advocate in a cage and let him out for periods of time. Tom Kelley of IDEO fame showcases the potential destruction of the Devil's Advocate run amuck. No one said this creature needs to live amongst you every day, but opening the cage door from time to time is both terrifying and helpful.

7. Use approaches other than discussion or face-to-face to make decisions. The Nominal Group technique or the Delphi Method offer opportunities to reduce the impact of group biases. Adopting a Six Thinking Hats (Edward DeBono) style of discussion management is a powerful method for eliminating the gunk from group discussions.

8. Constantly teach your group to both assess their decisions and improve their decision-making processes. This is a never-ending task of the effective leader.

9. Resist your natural tendency to assert your opinion. John Chambers at Cisco described this as one of the most critical issues in transforming from a command and control culture to one of collaboration. His traditional habit was to share his opinion of the answer to a problem after only a few minutes of group discussion. Of course, once he offered his opinion, all further creativity was stifled. Develop the discipline to extract opinions from others and be very, very careful when sharing your thoughts. If you are in a power position, your thoughts carry a great deal of weight, not because they are right, but because you have the power.

10. Reward, don't shoot messengers and failed experimenters. Remember Deming's point number 8: "Eliminate fear in the workplace." Live it.

11. Create and teach a risk framework. What's the worst that will happen? Can we bear the worst? If we cannot bear the worst, what can we change to reduce the worst? While many will argue appropriately that a good risk framework is much more involved, you can do worse than start with these three questions.

The Bottom-Line for Now:

Ultimately, your career and your company hinges on the decisions that you and others around you make. Given the broader forces affecting us all... speed, globalization, the march of technology and an exciting spread of diversity in our workplaces, this process of making decisions won't get any easier. You need to wake up every morning and walk in the door prepared to find a way to improve as a decision-maker while teaching others to do the same.

Chapter 50

Groupthink and Your Team

Groupthink is one of the nefarious decision-making challenges of teams, and a trap that many smart people and groups have fallen victim to throughout history. Learning to recognize the early warning signs is critical to keeping Groupthink at bay.

From the classic example cited in nearly every discussion on decision-making, the Kennedy administration's Bay of Pigs fiasco, to Ford's launch of the Edsel, to Neville Chamberlin's inner circle that believed peace with Hitler was at hand, Groupthink played a major role in some really bad decisions.

And while you might not be planning an invasion or negotiation with evil dictators or planning on launching an ugly automobile, chances are that Groupthink shows up from time-to- time in your professional world.

Recognizing Groupthink in the Workplace:

The essence of this decision-making trap is the irrational pursuit of consensus above all other priorities. Along the way, those who study group dynamics have identified a number of technical characteristics of Groupthink, including: suppression of reality testing, censorship of doubts, ignoring outside information, overconfidence and an emerging attitude of invulnerability. While some of these terms have a distinct technical ring to them, they are descriptive enough to suggest a closed, insular and out-of-touch with reality team culture.

I see Groupthink at work regularly on management teams that have convinced themselves that their strategy is the only way forward. They spend months defining a universe that fits their collective frame of reference, and then they build plans to operate in that universe. While the plans are often elegant, the team's construct on the external world and clients becomes as much fiction as fact, guaranteeing failure. After a long period of time invested in framing this strategy, Groupthink's cousin, Escalation of Commitment, joins the party and together, they work to block out evidence to the contrary and prevent the team from recognizing the need to restart.

Functional groups are prone to Groupthink when the organization's culture and structure emphasizes rigid boundaries and provides strong penalties for stepping on turf and toes outside of the group. As a survival (or coping) strategy, the isolated group begins to define the internal and external world from its own viewpoint. It shuts out external opinions and blocks ideas that are potentially threatening to the prevailing views and silo rules.

And perhaps more commonplace, project groups of all types often start to believe that achieving consensus is the only way to move forward on an issue. Often, if you peel a layer back on the push towards consensus, it's driven in large part out of an irrational concern for the feelings of others. "We want people to feel invested," or, "I don't want to step on anyone's toes." If this were the holiday season, I would offer a distinct, "Humbug!" The pursuit of consensus gives rise to the tyranny of mediocrity. Or worse.

Six Steps to Avoid Groupthink on Your Teams:

1. Anticipate Groupthink in your risk planning. While it might sound like planning to fail, it's good planning to identify a very real risk. And like any risk plan, there must be processes for monitoring and mitigating emerging Groupthink.

2. Size counts when it comes to teams. Limit the typical team size to less than 10 and ensure that there are well-defined boundaries for inclusion. Porous team boundaries and casual involvement of part-time team members creates a ripe environment for the irrational pursuit of consensus.

3. Invite external perspectives at various stages of the process. Of course, you've got to have the procedures in place to both protect external viewpoints and to find ways to incorporate them into the group's thinking and plans.

4. Lengthen the discussion phase before making a decision. Use structured discussion to focus on vetting the issues. Delay a rush to judgment. I encourage groups to incorporate non-typical discussion processes such as De Bono's *Six Hats Thinking* to dramatically improve discussion quality.

5. Develop a radically different second solution. I referenced this approach in my book with Rich Petro, *Practical Lessons in Leadership*. Challenge your team to assume that management will reject their first solution. Develop very different second solution and be prepared to defend it.

6. Invite the Devil's Advocate to the party. While a designated Devil's Advocate is a contrived role and everyone knows it, at least someone will be throwing rocks at the group's beautiful picture.

The Bottom-Line for Now:

Decision-making is tough enough, and it grows in complexity when there are groups involved. Don't naively assume that your group of smart people is immune to the many pitfalls and missteps that dot the path towards a decision. Groupthink is like the common cold, and while there may not be a cure, there sure are some preventative measures that can help keep it at bay.

Chapter 51

Team Stuck in the Creativity Deep Freeze?

Try "Why Not?" to Start the Thaw

Without exception, the healthiest businesses that I work with are those that offer a workplace environment and atmosphere that encourages a free-flow of ideas ranging from outlandish to "I can't believe we didn't think of that before." It is part of the natural culture of the firm to think in terms of "What if?" and "Why not?"

C reativity is part of the fabric of firms that encourage a free-flow of ideas. You see, hear and observe it on display in all roles and at all levels. Whether by design or more by a natural evolution fed by leaders that share a similar sense of curiosity and a genuine interest in and respect for the ideas of their employees, the processes and practices of creativity flourish in these environments.

Alternatively, the less than healthy firms I encounter share many failure attributes, including a complete lack of creativity and creativity-inducing practices and processes. Walk into one of those firms and you sense it immediately. Spend some time there and the silence from the lack of creativity or the quiet compliance in response to leader mandated creativity is simply deafening. It's the corporate equivalent of being locked inside a sensory deprivation chamber.

If you have the misfortune to be stuck inside one of those unhealthy firms, or, better yet, if you have the good fortune to be stepping in to turn the firm around, you might start with focusing on reacquainting people with the philosophy of "the possible."

As an aside, I'm convinced that almost every person in a bad business has a store of ideas on improving things just waiting to get out. You can break the spirits of people through lousy leadership, but the brain keeps working and ideas flow internally, usually straight into the brain's deep freeze bin, waiting for a future thaw.

Suggestions for Waking the Creative Giant Hiding Inside Your People and On Your Team:

1. Start by using the two words, "Why not?" Environments where creativity has been bred out of the culture are filled with people used to understanding what they cannot do. It's your job to seize every opportunity to draw forth even the simplest of novel ideas and the "Why not?" approach is a helpful tool. Respond to the conditioned phrases of, "We can't," or "If we could," or my favorite, "That's not how we do it here," with "Why not?" and listen patiently as people stammer and struggle to come up with an answer to that question that even they believe.

2. Follow-up with, "How would you... ?" and then shut up and listen. Expect some silence in return as neurons start firing and long-dormant brain connections are made and people slowly realize you're asking them how THEY would do something.

3. Finish up with, "What do you need from me?" and expect to suffer through a minor period of disorientation as people process on the reality that you, the boss, the person in charge, the person that is supposed to tell them what to do, just turned the entire equation around. Expect some surprised smiles.

4. Loop back with positive feedback: pay attention, offer encouragement, add support where needed, and in this instance, use genuine, positive feedback blended with selective coaching to support the effort.

Add water and stir.

The Bottom-Line for Now:

I run into people all of the time who challenge my basic premise that creativity is rocket fuel for firms and leaders. When I raised the specter of an alternative form of leader identification, particularly useful for project teams, I took a pretty good beating on my blog. I recently met with a talented group of young professionals and I received some good-natured challenges as to why one might not be able to apply the creative processes of the design firm, IDEO, to almost any type of firm and environment. Thematically in many of my essays, I'm calling for a quiet revolution in how we lead, manage and run our businesses. The *experts* are quick to point out all of the reasons why these ideas might not work.

My response: "Why not?"

Chapter 52

Digging Out After the Brainstorm

There are many forms of ideation and all sorts of new tools available to facilitate web-based and remote brainstorming. The key question really is, what are you going to do with the output?

Imagine yourself in the following scene: You've just wrapped up a day of brainstorming with colleagues from all areas of your company. The ideas were flowing and so were the flip-chart markers. The day's hard work is reflected in dozens of flip charts stuck to the walls around the room, and the only things left on the snack table are a few granola bars (has anyone who makes those things ever tasted one?) and some bruised apples in a bowl. The table in front of you is filled with markers, post-its, note-cards, wrappers and partially empty drink glasses.

You view the mess as a sign of an active day, and the volume of charts around the room supports that notion. Now, all that's left to do is figure out where to go next with all of the ideas listed on the flipcharts. Sound familiar?

Many of you will recognize the scene and a number of you will recall the challenge of figuring out what to do with all of the input. More than likely, you were reminded mid-session of the critical follow-up work by a participant who asked, "What's going to happen with all of these ideas after the session?"

So, what do you do with your walls filled with ideas?

Six Fairly Big Ideas for Digging Out After the Brainstorm:

1. Plan for the post-session work ahead of time. Real value is created based on what happens after the brainstorming session. Planning must reflect administrative needs…the capture and repurposing of the flip-chart information, as well as the critical process of determining how to identify ideas to push forward.

2. Share the rough post-session plan with your participants ahead of time. A good number of brainstorming invitees have taken up residence in the "Show Me" state of mind. As a condition of their unfettered involvement, they are looking to you to show them or at least describe to them what will happen to their ideas. They've participated too many times in the mental gymnastics of providing input with no output, and they are tired of wasting their limited time.

3. Keep the creative process running post-event. Ask people to keep thinking and building on session ideas. Provide the summary output to everyone and encourage them to build on the ideas or develop new threads. Provide a way for input to be added and shared with others.

4. Use caution when facilitating idea selection activities. A common technique for identifying ideas to extend is to apply some form of in-session voting process. Typically, after the brainstorm has reduced to a trickle, the facilitator suggests a mechanism for voting on the ideas to explore at this time. More often than not, this is where the multi-colored sticky dots come into play. Each participant receives a certain number of dots (votes) and is free to distribute them across their favorite ideas or to place them all on one particular idea. At the end of the voting, the top two or three are selected for exploration. There are a variety of iterations of the sticky dot (Vegas Voting) approach, but all suffer from the same challenges:

- Brainstorming and selection are two very different sets of activities and I hate to let selection issues bias or impact the ideation process. Just the knowledge that people will be voting on ideas to pursue opens the door for all sorts of social biases to join the meeting.

- Those who offer ideas and those responsible for filtering ideas may be two different groups of people. (Yeah, I know…how undemocratic of me. I'm not sure where the rulebook says majority vote rules on idea selection.) There's little stake in voting…you simply place a dot or add your tick mark without being invested in the vote. The voting may be based on unclear or inconsistent understanding of the ideas generated in the session.

5. Improve the process of selecting ideas for exploration by extending the process of evaluation and idea development. (Hey, no one said this was supposed to be fast…just good.) I'll make the leap that the brainstorming topics were well defined in your pre-planning session, and the output focused around those questions. Without this focus, the selection process is an impossible or at least highly arbitrary affair.

One approach: redistribute the ideas after the session and encourage the participants to not only continue thinking about and building on the ideas, but to select one they believe best addresses the brainstorm theme and recruit others to help extend the idea. This willingness to invest time in recruiting others and in thinking through the idea (and its implications) puts some personal skin in the game. People passionate enough about a concept to work it out are much more convincing to me than people capable of placing a sticky dot on a flip chart or index card. And I can assure you the universe of ideas will be narrowed considerably to the limited number of ideas people are willing to invest time and effort developing.

6. Create an opportunity for people to come together to describe and yes, even pitch their extended ideas. While I don't discount political biases here, it's fairly easy to see someone pushing an agenda versus someone and some group pushing an idea. At the end of the day, someone or some group still has to say "Yea" or "Nea" on moving ahead. I propose to push that point in time out until the idea-sponsors are ready to ask for money. Once investment has entered the dialogue, you've made the leap from idea on paper to potential project. Of course, if you don't have a good mechanism for evaluating and selecting new project investments...you've got a new problem.

The Bottom-Line for Now:

It's good to find good ideas, but it's great to find good ideas that grow legs. The process of moving from ideation to action is awkward and filled with opportunities for mistakes. One way to improve the process of idea development and selection is to let people vote with their time. A group of individuals motivated enough to invest time in building out an idea is a group worth listening to.

Chapter 53
Detoxing Your Team

Most of us can recall working with someone that had such a strong, negative impact on the work environment that you could literally feel the emotional mood swing when this person walked into a meeting.

For some unknown reason, perhaps a karmic-imbalance in the universe, toxic co-workers have the unnerving and disconcerting tendency to be great survivors. They rule their teams like Tony Soprano rules his goons, and they manage the higher-ups with diplomatic skills that would make Bill Clinton blush. And they do all of this in broad daylight, while the people who work for and with them roll their eyes and hope not to fall into the toxic character's line of sight.

While it is easy to intuit that toxic employees are value destroyers, we've been short on hard data about the true impact that these individuals have on the work environment. Until now. The April 2009 Harvard Business Review summarizes a study by Christine Porath and Christina Pearson that offers insights into "How Toxic Colleagues Corrode Performance." Porath and Pearson polled several thousand managers and employees from a variety of U.S. companies about the impact of toxic people at work, and the results affirm what we've long suspected.

The Impact of Working with Toxic Colleagues:

- 48% decreased their work effort.

- 47% decreased their time at work.

- 66% said their performance declined.

- 78% said their commitment to the organization declined.

And so on.

What to Do About Toxic Employees:

- Some of the best advice I ever learned the hard way was, "fire the politicians." In one case earlier in my career, I was the enabler for this toxic individual, preferring to see only his strengths and talents and ignoring the havoc he created in the working environment. Ultimately, I learned to fire the toxic characters fast. The individuals that did not share and exhibit the values that we espoused or that ruled through intimidation were the first ones out the door, regardless of their capabilities. I've never regretted firing a toxic employee.

- Toxic employees don't make it easy for you to fire them. The best of the worst actually frighten their bosses into inaction, not through overt intimidation or threats, but through more subtle approaches. Remember, these are skillful politicians with the hearts and minds of gangsters, and they've convinced a lot of people about how valuable they are to the organization. A conscientious manager may find herself swimming against the tide of popular opinion from her peers or higher ups on this issue.

- Brace yourself for a fight, don't be intimidated and stick to your guns. It's easier to back down and the toxic employee is betting on this outcome. Like most thugs and bullies, they don't expect people to stand-up to them and fight back.

The Bottom-Line for Now:

I'm certain that I read "fire the politicians" somewhere, and I wish that I could provide attribution. Regardless, it's good advice, especially in these tough times when teams are shrinking and those left behind must be capable of performing at a high level. If you're on the edge about who should go, you will be well served to get the toxicity out.

Chapter 54

Learn to Manage Your Team's Rhythms

All teams and groups have a rhythm and natural energy for their tasks that ebb and flow based on a variety of factors, including personal, environmental and seasonal to name a few. As a leader, you should be aware of these cycles that are characterized by either intense creativity, outstanding productivity or on the other extreme, a slow, plodding march through the days and weeks as if everyone's feet were encased in clay.

I t's your job to help smooth out the highs just a bit and minimize the time spent in the lows. Good coaches pay attention to the rhythm of their people and teams and leverage their leadership tools to make appropriate adjustments.

A Great Example of Managing the Rhythm:

One client managed an intensive and exhausting trade show and event program from March to May and then again during September and October. Energy and creativity peaked 30 to 60 days in advance of "go" and fell off the cliff as people caught their breath for a few weeks after the end of each period after traveling and working extraordinary hours for long stretches of time.

This team's manager shifted her focus from one of support, encouragement and oversight in advance of the programs, to one that facilitated recovery, rejuvenation and reinvigoration at the close of the programs. The 2x per year awards events (low budget, pizza and laughs) were "don't miss" opportunities to share the fun, excitement and achievements and to poke some great natured fun at slip-ups. These events were produced and emceed by team members and team members began carrying cameras to capture "moments" that would ultimately make their way into the team-produced awards presentation.

Celebration in this example transitioned to a reflective period, where the benefit of recovery time created a natural opportunity for reflection, assessment and improvement. While this "team" of cross functional participants worked together only for the event programs, every member had a voice in suggesting strategic ideas to beat competitors and better reach customers and prospects as well as to improve internal execution. Year after year, the results improved, the costs shrunk and competitors were left guessing. Oh, and everyone involved had a riot.

Five Common Rhythm Management Mistakes of Managers and Ideas to Improve:

1. Treating people like machines: not recognizing the need for rejuvenation and reinvigoration. Manager, you are not the source of your team's motivation. Team energy derives from many sources…a shared cause, a sense of belonging, individual and group pride and so many places other than from your cajoling or disingenuous cheerleading.

2. Staying distant from the challenge and not truly understanding the nature and intensity of the work. The manager described above also took on distinct tasks and played her part in program execution. Her credibility was sky high because she was involved in the work, albeit, in a highly specific role that didn't interfere with others charged with executing this program. She supported and served in this instance.

3. Getting too close to the execution. This sends the signal that you don't trust your team members. There is a fine line between appropriate oversight and micromanaging. Don't cross it.

4. Focusing the lessons-learned on the negatives. Instead of managing program debriefs to the tune of "What did we do wrong?" try the "What should we do more of?" approach and watch the change in tone and creativity.

5. Forgetting to celebrate. Pizza, some printed certificates and widespread team involvement in picking favorite moments, iron-man/woman awards for most travel, most hours etc. and any other fun category that your team members can think of, go a long way to creating a shared bond and driving some healthy laughs.

The Bottom-Line for Now:

Regardless of the type of group you lead, it is up to you to understand the rhythm of your teams and manage the cycles to match the business needs. Master this and watch performance grow. Oh, and you'll likely have a lot more fun in the process of doing great things, and that is a good thing.

Chapter 55

Six Warning Signs that Monotony and Routine Have Taken Over

It happens to the best of us. Days turn into weeks and quarters and pretty soon you're stuck in a seemingly endless cycle of years, budgets and programs. It's easy to let the rhythm of your business lull you into something less than your nimble, energized and kick-ass self. For the love of all that is good in the world of work, learn to fight that feeling!

L et's face it, there's much about the world of work for many that is monotonous or at least fairly routine. It's easy in many roles to get lulled into the rhythms and routines of days, weeks and months. Wake-up, dress, get on the train, drink coffee, meet, talk, write, plan, meet some more and run to catch the express train home. Rinse and repeat.

Monotony and routine are the natural born killers of creativity and innovation. Like weeds invading a spring lawn here in the Midwest, these twin killers quickly overwhelm the healthy pursuit of better, new and different.

Good leaders are like good gardeners: both take preventive measures to minimize the opportunity for monotony and routine to take root. However, even the best lawn-maestros know that there will be some encroachment of unwanted pests and other destructive forces. Being ever vigilant, they are on the lookout for the first signs of trouble and stand ready to spring into action.

Six Signs that Monotony and Routine are Infecting and Impacting Your Team:

1. Cue the nonverbal cues: people that are engaged, excited and inspired show it in many ways. Their pace is quick, their voices strong and upbeat and their eyes and faces show interest and animation. Learn to pay attention to the body language of your team members...these cues rarely lie.

2. Accountability fades into acceptance. High performance teams impose their own self-policing mechanisms for performance. When a team member fails to meet team standards or to live up to team values, the group takes action and requires accountability. When this self-correcting system is not visible...and when poor or incomplete performance is grudgingly tolerated, you can reasonably guess that monotony and routine have taken root.

3. Fire watching becomes a cultural hobby. I've seen this many times in tired environments. Problems are treated like a fire burning in a wastepaper basket while people just sit there watching it. "Yep, that looks like a fire," says one person. "How can we be certain that is a fire?" asks another. "Maybe the boss wanted a fire in that can," intones another. "Yeah, you're right. We better not touch it. Besides, I don't think we're responsible for fires," adds the next. If fires are springing up and burning out of control without anyone taking action, something is wrong.

4. There's a lot of fighting and no playing. Great groups know how to fight and play well together. Tired, frustrated, bored groups just fight and then bicker about each other. Be sensitive to the bicker-o-meter in your organization and if it starts heading in the wrong direction, it's time to take action.

5. Beware when failure is met with resignation and acceptance instead of a healthy frustration supported by a redoubling of efforts. Engaged people and teams fight failure with energy and creativity.

6. Be concerned when new initiatives and goals are met with a swirl of nothing. Tired and cynical teams (symptoms of monotony and routine) tend to choose and ignore new initiatives, confident in the understanding that with a long enough period of inaction, the initiatives usually fade into the ether of other management blah blah. This passive-aggressive behavior is more common than you might think and is a definite indicator that you've got team trouble.

The Bottom-Line for Now:

Recognition is the first step on the road to recovery. Good managers and leaders do more than judge team performance by the numbers in a report. They tune in to the attitudes, behaviors and the myriad of other clues that indicate that monotony and routine have taken up residence. And then they take action.

Chapter 56
Seven Ideas to Help Leverage Different Perspectives on Your Team

One of the most common tripping points of both early-career and experienced leaders is assuming that people are looking at issues and drawing similar conclusions. A leader explains the issues, offers a rationale for her suggested actions, heads nod, a few questions are exchanged, and then she leaves the meeting satisfied that all is clear and people are on board. She is, of course, horribly wrong!

Ask three people to stare at the same rock and describe what they see and you're very likely to get three very different answers. In his wonderful book on creativity, *Thinkertoys,* Michael Michalko describes a scenario where two people might look down a city street and one would be in awe of the lighting and shadowing and the other is disgusted by the rubble, garbage and broken concrete.

I see this a great deal in my MBA classes, where experienced professionals read common articles or view the same video, yet observe very different issues and draw different conclusions.

Of course, we see this in the workplace all of the time where groups of individuals come together to solve-problems or identify ideas to exploit opportunities. Sometimes the different perspectives drive creative solutions and on many occasions, they create conflict. In the latter scenario, attempts to reduce or end conflict often end up in a series of compromises, that when assembled, fail to fit the original issue.

Seven Suggestions for Leveraging the Different Perspectives on Your Team:

1. Accept that initially, almost no one will see the situation the same way that you do. This important recognition allows you to facilitate a process that will clarify and enhance the picture for everyone.

2. Let people see the problem and discover potential solutions for themselves. Your power of observation is stronger than your power of explanation. For example, indicating that a step in the customer support process needs to be changed because of complaints is subject to debate and disagreement. Alternatively, listening to audio exchanges in the call center or observing transactions in a store are much more convincing. Observations offer clarity and create opportunities for Ah-Ha moments and ideas that may prove far superior to the initial solution.

3. If opportunities for observation aren't readily available, use stories and pictures to get your point across. Relate experiences or wrap problems in stories to take an otherwise sterile issue and make it real.

4. Recognize the need to let people catch up. When you approach someone on a topic, his/her mind is likely somewhere in a different galaxy than yours at that point in time. Your extra effort to both allow time for people to "galaxy jump" and your patience in providing context for a situation will improve the effectiveness of the communication process.

5. Encourage questions. Even if people are silent for a few seconds (seems like eternity), resist the urge to fill dead air with more content. Silence often equals processing…not lack of understanding.

6. If possible, ask people to think about a situation and come back at a later time and offer thoughts and ask more questions. If the situation is particularly difficult or political, use techniques that depersonalize the questions and comments, including advance submission or writing down thoughts and submitting them anonymously during meetings.

7. And most of all, don't take it personally when people don't immediately line up behind you. Your response at this peak point of confusion and disagreement will govern the health or dysfunction of the dialogue moving forward.

The Bottom-Line for Now:

The wonderful thing about working with others is the diversity of ideas and perspectives that can potentially be developed to solve problems and seize opportunities. While disagreement might seem like conflict, it is fertile ground for creation. Embrace it and leverage the varying viewpoints for your organization's benefit.

Chapter 57

How to Improve Your Team's Problem Solving Skills

The best learning opportunities in the workplace occur when individuals or teams come face to face with a vexing problem. These situations provide outstanding growth opportunities and a great chance to generate and implement innovative and creative solutions. Of course, the manager has to create and play by the right rules.

Unfortunately, there are still too many managers that rip the heart out of great learning and team building opportunities with their micro-managing ways. A good micromanager (oxymoron by design!) focuses on what you are doing, but a great one takes it a step further and requires you to do it his way. It is his way or the highway.

Micromanaging squelches opportunities for creativity and personal development and reduces the health of the overall working environment to a level that no amount of coffee and cheerleading can possibly repair. While you might read this and scoff at the notion that you would ever dictate to people how to do things, it is more common than you might think.

Are you a micromanager? If you are, you can be certain that your style is conditioning your teams to depend upon you for problem-solving ideas.

And while it might be a nice ego-stroke to have people seeking you out for your expertise, you're actually failing as a leader here.

I see this issue frequently in technical environments where brilliant architects and developers are promoted to lead teams and instead of leading, they continue to perform their old jobs, simply telling people what to do and how to do it. To these individuals, this is almost logical, since in their minds, they were promoted based on the strength of their technical acumen.

Curing the micromanaging ways of lousy or uninformed leaders is a big topic for a good number of essays, so for today, I'll focus on what you can start and stop doing to better promote creative, independent problem-solving on your team.

Suggestions for Helping Improve Your Team's Problem-Solving Abilities:

- **Under ordinary circumstances, YOU should not tell people how to solve a problem.** Work hard to avoid being prescriptive. Of course, under extraordinary circumstances such as a safety or life or death situation, this might not be possible.

- **Do focus on ensuring your team carefully and objectively frames a problem.** Framing errors are a common cause of lousy decisions. It is often beneficial to secure external perspectives to challenge the group's perspective on the problem at hand.

- **Ensure everyone understands the gravity of the problem.** A crisis for one person or team might be a nuisance for another person or team. Ensure that everyone understands the implications of the issue.

- **Don't shoot down ideas and solutions that are different than what you would prescribe.** Instead, ask questions and seek to understand how the approach will meet the goals.

- **Always challenge assumptions, not methods.** The assumptions underlying a problem-definition or proposed solution merit detailed scrutiny. Unless you're a researcher, you should be less concerned about methods than the underlying logic.

- **Encourage individuals and groups to gain external input and/or to compare their proposed solutions to those already in place in the market.** For product, service or market problems, benchmarking against competitors can quickly uncover mundane, me-too solutions.

- **Encourage individuals and teams to look in non-traditional places for ideas.** A famous example is how managers at Toyota studied the U.S. Supermarket industry to gain ideas on just-in-time inventory and production techniques. Another example comes from Southwest Airlines studying racing pit crews to gain ideas on cleaning, maintaining and turning planes around faster.

- **Screw up the courage to let people try things radically different than what your approach would be.** Provide support, and if failure occurs, see the next point.

- **Recognize that failure is part of the path to getting it right**. Instead of prosecuting for failures, figure out how to leverage the experience for learning and improvement.

The Bottom-Line for Now:

Seek to enculturate effective, collaborative and creative problem solving that does not involve you at the epicenter of every solution. When problems start getting solved without your involvement, you are starting to succeed as a leader.

Section 8

Timeless & Priceless Leadership Advice

You cannot learn to lead by reading a book. However, you can absolutely gain some valuable insights into the tools and practices you must master to develop as an effective leader. You can also gain inspiration. The essays in this section are perfect for individuals who have just enough experience to know that a little bit of help and a bit of inspiration and encouragement can offer a great deal of support for the tough journey ahead.

In workshops and seminars, I frequently poll audiences on whether their first role as a leader was an outcome of a well-defined advancement process, or, something that seemed a lot more like an accident. The gross majority of individuals indicate the experience was much closer to "accident" than it was a "designed plan." Perhaps not surprisingly, most of the "accidental leaders" indicate receiving little support in the way of training or coaching during their start-up role.

Whether you are an experienced leader starting up with a new team or a first-time leader (by accident or design), paying attention to some of the fundamentals highlighted in this section may spell the difference between success and failure.

Chapter 58

Respectfully Speaking, Your Respect for Others Will Serve You Well

The formula is simple and the outcome is predictable. Treat people with respect and they will generally return the courtesy many times over. Ditto on the opposite behavior.

The word "respect" just might work as the lone word in the world's shortest chapter in the world's shortest and most effective book on leadership. Master the term, practice it liberally and you've uncovered one of the secrets to leading effectively.

A fair number of leaders forget this lesson somewhere during their journeys and they squander countless opportunities every day to energize, inspire and engender loyalty. It's easy to grow lazy and whiff on this one. It takes discipline and diligence to apply it consistently. Oh, and don't confuse the concept of "respect" with anything that resembles being soft. You can and should hold people accountable, expect the best out of everyone and offer constructive feedback quickly and frequently. You can do all of this without being a jerk.

Seven Ideas to Improve Your Respect Rating:

1. Look people in the eye and listen attentively when they are talking with you. Yes, this means turning away from the e-mail that you are typing or holding off on glancing at and responding to the message on your blackberry.

2. Learn names and use them. A CEO that I worked for believed so strongly in this that he fired a factory general manager for failing to learn the names of the people on the floor. And while there were other issues, this was a critically important issue to the CEO. The GM had been warned. The CEO knew the names and then some after two visits.

3. Learn to deliver effective constructive and positive feedback. Feedback is great, personal attacks are never appropriate and most constructive feedback is never public. Use fact-based observation to discuss needed behavioral changes. Always link the behavior to business. Deliver your feedback supportively and clearly, and hold people accountable.

4. Pay attention to people. One of the easiest ways to reduce your Respect Rating is to fail to engage and get to know the people that work for you as human beings. While much about work life is transactional, the simple acts of noting pictures on a desk, asking about weekend activities or checking up on how things are going for difficult issues that were shared with you, are free and priceless all at the same time. Show genuine interest and you show respect.

5. Support the professional development of your team members. The ultimate form of respect you can pay someone is to support their efforts to develop and grow. Invest time and energy in helping someone gain experience or develop new skills and you'll have a willing and grateful supporter for life.

6. Make decisions and quit holding people and teams hostage. I worked next to a leader that equated making a decision on a new idea or program as tantamount to putting himself in front of the firing squad. His simple philosophy of, "If I'm not accountable for anything, I can't be fired," was fascinating and horrifying to watch all at the same time. He was fired.

7. Trust people. There are few better ways to show your respect than to trust people to do their jobs. Ask for help. Ask for their opinions and where possible, adopt their advice. If you can't trust your team members, you either have serious trust issues or, you've got the wrong people.

The Bottom-Line for Now:

We hungrily devour leadership content of all sorts, desperately looking for the unique insight or pearl of wisdom that will make things right for us as leaders. Ironically, the answer is in front of us, in the lesson that most of our parents and teachers taught us during our earliest years: treat people with respect at every encounter. Now is a great time to start.

Chapter 59

How to Grow Your Leadership Credibility in 15 Easy Lessons

Like good health, you cannot have too much credibility as a leader.

Too many leaders swim through their corporate and organizational lives oblivious to the reality that their actions, utterances, decisions and even the most casual of their interactions are all monitored, evaluated and voted upon every day.

The people who work for us cast mental votes assigning a positive or negative credibility rating (CR) that ultimately determines our ability to influence others. And while your CR can move over time, it tends to move quickly and irreversibly towards the negative and only very slowly towards the positive.

You build credibility as a leader one interaction and one decision at a time over a long period of time, and you destroy credibility in great and dramatic fashion almost instantaneously through what I characterize as Dumb Ass Maneuvers (DAMs). While we're all capable of mistakes, DAMs tend to reflect a series of mistakes or actions that cause people to question your intentions, wonder about your qualifications and speculate on your ethics. To optimize your credibility building and to minimize the probability of creating too many DAMs, consider my suggestions below.

How to Grow Your Leadership Credibility in 15 Easy Lessons:

1. Say what you mean and do what you say. Your do must match your tell.

2. Treat everyone with respect all of the time. Constantly. Always!

3. It's never about you. Strike "I" from your vocabulary.

4. Make and communicate decisions. And then work hard to teach others to make and communicate decisions.

5. Stop! Pay attention and listen. You show respect by paying attention.

6. Ask questions. Questions show that you care. Questions also teach others how to think.

7. Create and reinforce accountability. People actually prefer to be accountable versus the alternative. People respect accountability. Wield it liberally and consistently.

8. Develop your people. Your willingness to support the development of others speaks volumes about you as a leader.

9. Master feedback. Use it daily to support growth and promote accountability.

10. Teach. Leaders teach...practice this role more often than the role of a critic.

11. Create context for others. Communicate strategies and goals and help everyone connect their priorities to the firm's priorities.

12. Dispense all of the glory. Keep none of it for yourself. See number 3 above if this one doesn't make sense.

13. Admit your mistakes. Quickly. Highlight the lessons learned and move on. Never, ever hide mistakes or attempt to transfer responsibility.

14. Hire smart people that share your firm's values. Then, respect the intelligence that you've hired by working to create an atmosphere where your smart people can focus on doing great things.

15. Be authentic. Be yourself and don't be afraid to let people see you for who and what you are...a fallible human interested in doing your best for your team members and for your organization.

The Bottom-Line for Now:

Credibility is the leader's best friend. It's also the leader's source of motive power. Grow it, guard it and use it in good health to build great teams, great businesses and great professionals.

Chapter 60

Getting it Right When Starting Up with Your New Team

Stepping into the role of new (to the team) leader for an existing team is a daunting task. It's also a time rich in opportunity for everyone involved if the new leader executes a proper start-up strategy and avoids the most common start-up pitfalls.

A Start-Up is a Horrible Thing to Waste:

Regardless of your background and success, teams tend to view the new leader with a bit of healthy cynicism. You're the newbie, and you haven't done anything yet to earn the respect of the current team members. Manage the process properly, and high performance might just come your way. Get it wrong, and you squander a precious opportunity.

The 4-Stages of New Leader Assessment:

1. Doubt and Uncertainty
2. Hope
3. Belief
4. Trust

Your goal is to move quickly beyond the cloud of Doubt and Uncertainty to Hope and then on towards Belief. Trust is something that comes much later, usually after a lot of reinforcement and after individual team members have engaged and benefitted in some form from your leadership support.

Fair warning, many new leaders start shooting themselves in both feet from the moment they open their mouths for the first time, and end up destroying any possibility of progressing through the stages. Once Doubt and Uncertainty turn to Cynicism and Disregard, it's all over for you with this team.

5 Key Issues at Start-Up:

1. You must understand the business mission of your team and how it fits into the bigger picture of your firm's strategy. You owe your team context for their purpose and for their work. Reinforcing (or building) the linkages between team priorities and organizational priorities is a key task of a leader. Of course, you need help from your boss, your peers and your internal and external customers to gain this context for yourself. Your networking, questioning and listening skills are critical in this pursuit.

2. It's time to break the ice. Help the team get to know you...and of course, you've got to get to know the team members as individuals and as role players. In both group and one-on-one settings, you've got to ask and execute on these questions:
- What's working?
- What's not?
- What do you need me to do?

The first two create content ripe for group assessment and action. The third one opens the door to identifying opportunities for you to knock down walls and accelerate your movement through the stages.

3. Identify opportunities to help the team while quietly assessing performance and talent. You won't know this team and the people for a while and unless there are raging people problems, resist a rush to judgment. I tend to begin realigning new teams very carefully at around the 45-day mark, with a target to have this part of the job completed by day 90. Your actions here must be preceded by a great deal of observation and listening.

4. Begin forming an effective working atmosphere based on accountability, transparency, fairness and a propensity towards action. Once you break the ice and get people talking about key issues and obstacles, you can support their efforts to deal with the issues. Establish accountability and standards for quality from the start and don't let go of these key issues. Identify opportunities to support the development of your team members.

5. Begin to turn your attention to professional development issues. Within the 90-day window, but somewhere beyond the first 30 days, it's appropriate to add to your list of questions above: What do you want to do here?

For those team members going forward with you, you owe it them and to yourself to provide developmental opportunities that allow people to explore their desired directions.

4 Common Pitfalls of the Start-Up Leader:

1. Making it all about you. You've invaded their world…it's truly all about them, not you.

2. Asserting without context for the team and its' mission or for the culture and values of the team. Again, it's their team…until you've earned the right to say "my team" or better yet, "our team."

3. Imposing your way and will instead of helping the team understand the need for a new way.

4. Operating with a hidden plan. "The Secret Plan" didn't help President Nixon engender trust when talking about unraveling the Vietnam conflict, and not talking about the expectations from your boss for the team engenders doubt and cynicism. (Note to my readers: I may be showing my age with the Nixon comment here. I was only 7 when he uttered those words, and I didn't believe him then.)

The Bottom-Line for Now:

For a brief moment in time as you start-up as the new leader of an existing team, you have a remarkable opportunity to make a difference. You get one shot at working your way through the 4-Stages. Don't squander the opportunity by tripping all over yourself.

Chapter 61

Strengthen as a Leader by Developing as a Follower

It took me a long time to recognize that followership and leadership are inextricably linked. Developing as both leader and follower is critically important in a world where leadership is fluid and it's common to serve as leader for one initiative and follower/participant for others.

I grew up to the refrain of, "Be a leader, not a follower," and the drive to lead is part of who I am. Part and parcel of this was a resistance through much of my early career to the idea that, "to be a good leader, you need to be a good follower."

For me, and I know for many others, our ambition is to drive change, right wrongs and challenge the status quo and to advance. Mentally, it's hard to connect those core professional drives with the passive and even weak sounding notion of "following."

I didn't buy the "be a good follower" story for quite awhile in my career, and in discussions with many emerging leaders, they struggle with this concept as well. A common theme I hear emphasizes the association of and confusion around the significant difference between being a good follower versus blindly following someone. The two are very different, and serving as a good follower absolutely has nothing to do with suspending your own judgment, stifling your views on right or wrong or becoming visible as that most odious of corporate characters, the "Yes-Man."

It's time to put a positive light on followership as a prelude to effective leadership and to offer some guidance for those seeking to advance their leadership careers.

Common Misnomers About Followership:

- Being a good follower is about nodding your head and supporting your boss regardless of your own beliefs.

- Following equals weakness.

- Being a good follower means that you must suspend your own judgment.

- Being a good follower requires blind and mute obedience.

- You're a bad follower if you challenge your boss.

- Followership is a euphemism for playing politics.

- Followership requires you to focus on supporting someone over the organizational good.

My reaction to all of the above is a resounding: Wrong!

Six Ways to Grow and Develop as a Follower Without Compromising Your Integrity:

1. Seek first to understand. Proactively seek to understand organizational goals and strategies as well as the personal/professional goal and priorities of the people that you work for. Any gaps between the two are opportunities for you to engage with your boss and others to ensure proper organization, team and individual focus.

2. Develop curiosity, but don't forget the tact. Choose the right opportunities to ask questions, seek clarity, and professionally and politely challenge assumptions and share alternative viewpoints. The good leader values these habits in her followers.

3. Become an active citizen in your manager's world. Don't confuse this with compromising your ethics or morals. However, it's critical to recognize that someone chooses you for success. The "someone" is usually your boss. Learn and live the laws, rules and customs of society as defined by your boss.

4. Recognize that politics, power and influence are not dirty words. It is naïve to ignore these ever-present facets of organizational life. Engage in the activities ethically and professionally. Work hard to develop strong coalitions and use your influence to move your team's and your manager's programs forward.

5. Don't let the boss run around naked. With grace, courtesy and haste, tell the Emperor when he is walking about sans clothing. A good follower is also a good protector.

6. Seek first to understand, part 2. Even poorly delivered feedback contains nuggets of gold. Many managers lack technique and training for supporting your development. While you might interpret a poorly constructed feedback comment as unfounded criticism, it may very well be your manager's best attempt at helping you improve. Resist the anger you may feel and seek the wisdom behind the muddled message.

The Bottom-Line for Now:

We all follow someone in the workplace, and ignoring the need to become an effective follower is tantamount to shooting yourself in the foot. Your mind says, "get out of my way and let me lead," but reality says that you need to coexist. The challenge is to coexist without compromising your ethics, values and your integrity. Easy words to say, but a difficult balancing act to achieve. As you grow as a leader, you'll come to recognize your dependence upon good followers, and you will appreciate those that follow with positive intentions, untarnished morals and a strong desire to help you, the team and the organization succeed.

Chapter 62

The Feedback on Feedback

There are no silver bullets in leadership, but feedback comes darned close.

Over the past several years, I've made a professional hobby out of exploring the fascinating and very real fear that so many people have for delivering constructive feedback. One of my favorite interviews was with a retired CEO, who when I posed the question on whether he had any regrets, without hesitating, responded: *"I really regret that I never learned how to have the tough discussions with the people that worked for me."* He quickly added, *"To this day, I wonder how much money that I cost my companies."*

While many readers may be quick to conclude that this gentleman made it to CEO without mastering the fine art of feedback, my pushback is that good enough isn't good enough, especially when you are talking about a skill set in the C-Suite that can dramatically impact the organization's working environment and ultimately, overall performance. It's quite possible the inability to master feedback kept this CEO and his organizations from becoming great. Good isn't good enough when great is in sight.

My informal approach to researching the topic of feedback would not qualify as a well designed study, however, I'm pretty comfortable extrapolating the results to the broader population. By the way, my informal sample size is approaching 2,000 people from all types of organizations and at all levels of leadership.

My Feedback on Feedback:

- A majority of respondents indicate never receiving any formal training on feedback.

- A majority of experienced managers answering my anonymous surveys describe delivering negative feedback as one of their major weaknesses.

- Most leaders are not evaluated on their feedback skills and effectiveness.

- A majority of respondents indicate that they frequently delay delivering tough feedback. The exception is for situations where safety or security are involved.

- A majority of respondents indicate that they feel better about delivering constructive feedback if they deliver praise at the same time. (Note: this sugarcoating or sandwiching is one of my pet peeves. For anyone interested, check out the essay, "Why I Hate the Sandwich Technique for Delivering Feedback.")

- And in a carry over from the earliest surveys on this topic, a gross majority of respondents indicated they wish that their managers were better at delivering feedback.

I've expanded my inquiries on feedback to the world of informal leaders (Project Managers in particular), and the feedback on feedback here is equally challenging. These professionals are definitely not trained on feedback, and they clearly recognize the impact that their lack of comfort with this tool has on their ability to deal with troubled project teams.

And finally, with a keen eye and ear for the "F" issue inside organizations, when I am called upon to help struggling firms and teams with strategy or other performance issues, it is a safe bet that the feedback culture is unhealthy. Discussions may be collegial, but they don't focus on the real performance issues of people and teams.

Why Do We Fear Feedback?

Marshall Goldsmith offers up a great perspective (I paraphrase): *There's only two things wrong with providing successful people with feedback. They don't want to hear it from us and we don't want to give it to them.*

It's a human thing. We fear negative reactions. We are overly concerned that people won't like us if we criticize them. The CEO example described earlier was worried that he would create a negative working environment, and he didn't want to damage whatever team and one on one credibility existed in that environment.

The fears are all understandable. I suspect that every one of us can empathize with the source of those fears. We just need to move beyond them.

The Power of Feedback:

There are no silver bullets in leadership, but feedback comes darned close. Used properly, this is the leader's most powerful tool for promoting and strengthening positive behavior and for identifying and improving less than desirable behaviors.

High quality professionals...the type you want to surround yourself with, want and appreciate effective feedback. For teams and individuals that perform at acceptable levels, feedback can help them move from good to great. Feedback, as Ken Blanchard says, *"Is the Breakfast of Champions."*

Conquering the Fear and Cultivating Your Feedback Skills:

My own experience training hundreds on this topic has shown that once people understand the power of this leadership tool, mastering it includes:

- Learning to construct complete, behaviorally focused and business-oriented feedback messages.

- Learning to deliver these messages in a frank, respectful and effective (concise, timely, brief) manner.

- Understanding how to manage even the toughest of discussions.

- Setting the stage for active coaching and more feedback on the behaviors in question.

- Practicing using a "system" that incorporates all of the above. Practice, and more practice, and then some more. Of course, the gross majority of the practice is in a live fire setting.

The Bottom-Line for Now:

This most difficult of human interactions in the workplace is also one of the most important. The fear, much like the fear of public speaking, is mostly in our minds. With some deliberate practice, all of us are capable of improving our skills, and as a result, improving our performance, the performance of our teams and of our organizations. It's time to move beyond the fear.

Chapter 63

Why I Hate the Sandwich Technique for Delivering Feedback

At the risk of inviting the ire of a great number of readers and trainers, I am once again opting for the dissenting opinion on a controversial topic. I absolutely hate the use of the "sandwich" technique in delivering constructive feedback.

For those of you that need a memory jog, the *Sandwich Technique* is the approach that many trainers suggest for delivering constructive feedback-the developmental kind, not the positive kind. It involves delivering praise, offering the specific constructive criticism and then closing off with more praise. The criticism is "sandwiched" between two points of praise.

Many find this approach comfortable. It allows for an easy discussion opener and takes away from some of the fear of diving into the real behavioral issue.

Given that many, many managers struggle to conduct the tough feedback discussions due to various (irrational) fears: fear of offending, fear of not being liked, fear of losing someone, fear of upsetting working dynamics, the *Sandwich Technique* offers a security blanket. Those teaching the technique argue that at least it facilitates having the discussion, and that is better than not having it. While I am a huge advocate of delivering timely feedback, I'll take mine without the bread please.

5 Reasons Why the Sandwich Technique is a Truly Bad Practice:

1. It is a crutch that is solely for the benefit of the giver, not the receiver.

2. It obfuscates the real message.

3. It confuses the receiver by watering down the key message.

4. It destroys the value of positive feedback by linking it with the negative. Don't forget that positive feedback is a powerful tool for reinforcing the right behaviors and the sandwich technique devalues this tool.

5. It is insulting to the receiver and borderline deceitful. "Bob, you did a great job on XYZ, but... ." It's like a pat on the back followed by a sucker punch followed by another pat on the back.

Less Bread, More Meat:

- Overcome your fear of delivering constructive feedback by planning your discussions, and importantly, planning and practicing your discussion openers by getting politely and clearly to the point.

- Follow the single-behavior/single discussion rule.

- Ensure that you are focusing on the behavioral issue.

- Link the issue to business impact.

- Identify the proper and required behavioral change.

- Jointly develop a plan to drive the change.

- Follow up to discuss progress and next steps.

The Bottom-Line for Now:

Consider this some robust feedback: quit sugarcoating your performance discussions. Your associates will respect you more for your clarity and your support of their development. It's time to grow up and lead.

Chapter 64

Your Journey from Fear to Self-Confidence

In spite of the popular myth of the fearless leader, it is my belief that a large number of leaders at all levels struggle with fear. Some work through their fears on the way to developing self-confidence and others battle it daily and resort to various coping strategies, including over-compensating with extreme aggression or extreme timidity.

L earning to positively and productively cope with fear is an important part of developing as a leader. Fear is palpable for humans, and those placed in positions of responsibility for leading others share the same issues as the rest of the population. Showing fear and vulnerability in the workplace is perceived as something to be avoided at all costs for all employees, and doubly so for those in leadership roles. Nonetheless, it exists.

Common Fears of Leaders:

- **Early career leaders are often giant bundles of unspoken fears** where everything is foreign and guidance is often nowhere to be found. They perceive that they are responsible for everything, yet they don't know how to do anything.

- **Many individuals worry that it will be discovered that they are actually bluffing their way through their days.** They fear being outed as frauds to their team members and their bosses. There are often two different groups for this one. There are the conscientious individuals that are learning on the job and that few would perceive as disingenuous. And then there are those that truly don't get it and as a result, they adopt bluster and bravado as their best friends.

- **Many leaders fear specific tasks such as delivering feedback, dealing with personal and team conflict,** interacting with senior management or getting up in front of the entire company to provide an update. The common response to these issues is avoidance.

- **Fear of losing power drives some leaders to engage in all manner of destructive or at least counter-productive activities** in an attempt to strengthen their hold on their slice of the kingdom.

- **Fear of making decisions is often driven by political fear** or the fear of being visible as having been "wrong," and the result is an unwillingness to take risks and make decisions.

I could go on, but I'm at risk of practicing psychology without a license here, so let's move to some solutions and coping strategies. A quick note… for those of you reading this far and looking forward to me launching on the evil leaders, you'll have to wait for another day. The suggestions below are focused on helping well-intentioned professionals and leaders learn to cope with, overcome, or at least harness their fears for productive use.

Five Suggestions for Overcoming Common Fears:

1. Dealing with anxieties around "what to do?" You need to accept the reality that one of the key challenges and opportunities of leading comes from dealing with ambiguity. On the one hand, there is often not a clear way forward, so you are on your own or at least on your own with your team members to figure it out. The good news is that no one else knows the absolute right answer for most situations, including your boss or the CEO. Seek out the best information given the circumstances, involve your team members in developing ideas and approaches and help everyone move forward. If you've made a mistake, work with the team and take corrective action based on the lessons learned.

2. Dealing with the anxiety of, "I'm not sure how to lead." Regardless of how your role as a leader came about, someone somewhere observed something in you beyond just a heartbeat, so quit worrying about how you got there and start focusing on learning the role. Know your role, align your priorities around helping, enabling and supporting your team members and don't look back. While we are born with various attributes that might help or hinder our leadership skills, in my opinion, most leaders are made. The only way to learn to lead is by leading.

3. Overcoming fear of feedback. It's widely understood that the ability to deliver constructive, behavioral focused feedback is one of the most important tools and activities of a leader. It's ironic, that in surveys and workshops, this activity is consistently identified as a personal weakness. Why?

People fear negative reactions, they fear suddenly not being liked or respected, or they lack the self-confidence to politely assert on the behaviors and actions required for the mission. Ironically, employees generally value respectful behavioral feedback and grow frustrated when they don't receive it.

4. Overcoming your fears is best accomplished through a combination of study and practice. There are ample sources on learning the very logical and simple approaches to delivering feedback and dealing with conflict or, on overcoming the fear of speaking in public. Take the time to learn the processes and best and worst practices and then go out and put this knowledge to work. The directions to Carnegie Hall are still the same: practice, practice, and more practice.

5. Dealing with a fear of making decisions. You will be wrong. Probably more often than you would like to consider. Now get over it. The only thing worse than making a wrong decision is holding your team hostage by never making a decision.

I encourage and mentor young leaders on simple decision-making and risk analysis models and like any of the skills-based fears, as you add some context and structure to your thinking and then practice the activity in live-fire settings, your confidence will quickly expand.

The Bottom-Line for Now:

Facing up to your fears is an important part of growing up and succeeding. Ultimately, you will need to develop the right balance of self-confidence tinged with fearlessness and wrapped in a bit of humility to succeed.

Teams smell and sense fear and that breeds uncertainty in the working environment. On the other hand, teams and individuals sense bluster and bravado and that is destructive as well. Learn to confront your fears head on and seek out the tools and training necessary to hone your skills. Then, put this to work and recognize that no one expects you to be perfect...but everyone expects you learn, grow and improve and to help them do the same. As you overcome your fears, remember to pay it forward.

Chapter 65

Two Voices on: The Words of Leaders

A note from Art: This dual post was the outcome of a casual exchange of thoughts via Twitter that quickly evolved into a must-write piece and fun collaboration. My partner in crime here is Mary Jo Asmus, a wonderful and thoughtful writer, accomplished executive coach and business consultant. You can find Mary Jo's great leadership content and her coaching services at: www.aspire-cs.com

A note from Mary Jo: Through twitter conversations and a telephone discussion about the importance of the words a leader speaks, we came to this place of deciding to collaborate on an essay about the topic. Through the lens of differing, but complementary aspects of a leader's words, we found that the collaboration worked to produce the following post that we not only had some fun putting together, but helped us to learn a thing or two from each other.

The Words of a Leader-Mary Jo Asmus

"We are what we think. All that we are arises with our thoughts. With our thoughts, we make the world." Buddha

"Thoughts become words. Words become actions. Actions become character. Character is everything." Unknown

"Think before you speak." Mom

The Buddha, Unknown, and Mom were all very smart. They knew that all words arise from thoughts, and that the words we speak have the power to build, inspire, create, or destroy. Before your words are formed and spoken, there is a time of thought. The thought that creates the words might be only a nanosecond. But this little bit of time can't prevent you from saying something that was unintended or might be taken out of context. And because followers tend to be hyper vigilant about their leaders, anything you say has a greater effect than you may be willing to believe.

So this is the connection that all leaders need to be aware of. Thoughts become words that become actions. To say the right things to take the right actions, you may need to begin with your thoughts.

Change Your Thoughts, Change Your Words;

In our speed-of-light world, you must slow down to become aware of your thoughts, to speak and take action in a way that is congruent with your values. You can bet that successful athletes imagine and rehearse successful outcomes before following through on them. Why wouldn't this apply to you and the words you use as a leader? What successful outcomes do you want your words to speak of?

Imagine using words that will build, inspire, and create. What are they? Imagine your words being accepted and used in the way you intend them to be. Consider the values you hold most dear. What are your values, and how will your words describe them? How will they be incorporated into the language you use every day?

Take a mental break from the anxiety, worry, and judging that goes on in your thoughts. Consider using a reflective or a meditative practice that will allow you to do this. Just as an athlete must rest his muscles, it also makes sense for you to rest your mind and thoughts. Such a practice has the effect of slowing you down, allowing you to renew yourself at the level of thought. If you notice your thoughts as they arise in your practice, you'll have begun a process of observing that puts you on a path to improving the words you speak as you go about your everyday life. A reflective or meditative practice has arms that reach far beyond the minimal time you spend doing it.

Where your thoughts don't serve you, change them. Negative self-talk around guilt, anger, or hatred won't help you say the words that your followers need to hear. When those thoughts arise, ask yourself if they are serving you as a leader. If they aren't, what would you prefer to change them to?

Your thoughts come through in your words, even if you don't realize it. You can be sure that others do. Become aware of your thoughts, and your words can be intentional, purposeful, and life giving. You will then find it easier to accept the wise suggestions of my colleague, Art, below.

The Words of a Leader-Art Petty

I've often marveled at the speed that an off-handed comment from the boss can fly through an organization, quickly evolving into policy or direction. "Mary said..., ," or, "I just heard that... ." Have you had the unfortunate experience of seeing or hearing a manager publicly chastise a subordinate? This abuser seems to take strength from the assertion of power while the receiver visibly shrinks in stature. Observers feel pity for one and anger at the other.

Have you had the good fortune to work for someone that seemed to draw the best out of you through constructive coaching and encouragement? This type of an impact can last a lifetime.

Have you wondered what it is about that manager that everyone wants to work for? The comments usually go something like this: "She's demanding and holds us accountable, but we're accomplishing things and having fun in the process."

A License to Talk:

While the communication process comprises much more than just the words that we string together, the words truly serve to build-up people, teams and organizations. Words inspire, motivate, challenge, teach and encourage. Or, they serve as the blunt force weapons of personal and professional trauma and destruction.

Good leaders are builders and they form and shape their words into phrases and questions that encourage learning, improvement, risk-taking and more learning. Good leaders are master craftsmen in many ways, and words are some of their most important tools.

Less effective leaders use words like tools as well, but in this case they crassly apply the words of brute force in settings where precision is called for. They use the end of a wrench to pound in a nail, and seem to disregard the damage to the surrounding area. Of course, they should have used a finishing hammer and a nail set.

Other leaders use words to shape agendas. Good politicians broker understanding and alliances through their words. Less well-intentioned leaders use words to sew the seeds of doubt and mistrust and to shape alliances that benefit one person or one team.

Words are powerful tools. Perhaps leaders should be trained and certified on their use. Hmmm. Perhaps leaders should be trained in general, much as a master craftsperson would train an apprentice.

Sticks and Stones:

I doubt that many of us have spent a lot of time considering our approach to word-choice much since our playground days, where the use of words as weapons by some is first mastered. The defense of, "Sticks and stones will break my bones but names will never hurt me," was never really a good defense, was it?

While many of us intuitively understand how powerful our words are, in my own experience, we do a less than effective job teaching this to our apprentice leaders. Consider how many "coaching opportunities" are created as we deal with teams and individuals that push back based on the "approach" used by these early leaders. Peel away the issues and at the bottom, you'll almost always find an issue with words.

There's no manual for this topic, but perhaps a few well-intended "words" will help. Consider sharing this with your apprentice leaders and perhaps you'll avoid the "he said/she said" coaching calls in favor of something more constructive.

Words of Advice:

- Listen more than you talk. Use your words sparingly. Leading doesn't mean that you are required to talk more than anyone else. Quite the opposite.

- Think before you talk. Choose your words deliberately.

- A well-turned question is often more effective to get people thinking than a dozen statements. Manage your questions to comments ratio.

- All of your words must include respect as a foundation. As soon as respect is left out of your words, you've lost.

- Make certain that your words and your body language match. Given a choice between the two, studies indicate that people believe the body language over the words.

- Tough conversations on performance are part of your job. Embrace this reality and don't sugarcoat your words. Do keep them focused on behaviors and keep the behaviors linked to business.

- Genuine words of encouragement and well-deserved words of praise are rocket fuel for individuals and teams.

- "The do must match the tell." The words of leaders not backed by actions and support are just hot air.

- Be aware that your words as a leader will be amplified and distorted. Manage your words carefully.

The Bottom-Line on The Words of a Leader:

The choice is yours to lead like a master craftsman or a common hack. Choose and use your words carefully and you'll be amazed at what those around you create.

Chapter 66

How Can I Help?

"How can I help?"

These four simple words are powerful leadership tools
when applied with genuine intent.

The leader who is comfortable asking this question is comfortable in his or her leadership skin. It takes self-confidence, a dose of humility and a genuine comprehension of the role of leader to form and apply the question, "How can I help?" This individual understands that "telling" isn't the only way to lead.

The act of asking the question shows that the leader has confidence in his team members. This is a subtle but important way for the leader to say, "I trust you" to individuals and teams.

The Intent of "How Can I Help?"

The engineering manager asking this question isn't expecting to be invited to lead the next design review or to write a few lines of code. She wants to know if she can provide support by providing resources, helping to shape policy, brokering alliances and repairing systemic problems. **She's really asking:**

- Are there obstacles in your way that I can clear out for you?

- Do you have the tools and resources that you need to do the work?

- Is there something wrong with our business processes that we can improve?

- Is there something that I can do that will increase the likelihood that teams and individuals will succeed?

Don't confuse the use of "How can I help?" with the need to pitch in on the loading dock so that customers receive their orders or the need to sit in on a team meeting where the group has been unable to work well together. These types of situations provide context for the leader to truly help. The individual acts are just part of the bigger picture problem-solving process.

The Bottom-Line for Now:

Don't discount how much self-confidence it takes for a leader to ask the question, "How can I help?" Much of modern leadership culture is predicated on the false belief that those at higher levels are paid to tell people how and what to do. Just like "telling ain't teaching," it's usually not leading either.

Section 9
In Pursuit of Greatness

The great leaders in our lives leave lasting imprints. They change our lives for the better by inspiring us, challenging us and sometimes, by metaphorically kicking us in our rears to get going. Great leaders are strivers, dedicated to their profession and committed to doing everything possible to support their people, their teams and their organizations. Fortunately for all of us, developing as a great leader is within reach. It's not easy, but frankly, the recipe is not locked in the vault along with the formula to Coca Cola. In fact, it's fairly straightforward.

The formula for achieving greatness as a leader simply requires strong self-awareness, unyielding commitment, sheer tenacity and a healthy dose of humility. Blend those qualities with a willingness to take chances on the talent around you, a great attitude on learning from mistakes, and a need for fearlessness in the face of adversity, and you're almost there. Mix the ingredients above, apply liberally and work at it for a career, and you might just pull this off.

This section is for those who believe that good isn't good enough, especially when greatness is within reach.

Chapter 67

Trying Not to Fail is Not the Same as Striving for Success

*There's a definite difference between focusing on
not failing versus striving for success.*

When we focus on not failing, fear rents most of the space in our mind, and we see monsters in need of slaying everywhere we turn. We lose track of the original vision that propelled our actions, and the sheer act of working becomes at best a passionless exercise and at worst, drudgery.

Lousy Leaders Thrive on Your Misery:

Sadly, many leaders provide fuel for the "don't fail" machine through their actions. Show me a project team or functional group that exhibit all of the energy and passion of a collection of late-night television zombies, and I'll guarantee there's one or more tyrannical, micro-managing leaders at the source of the dysfunction.

The Scarlet "F

The "don't fail" disease isn't limited to the corporate world. I know small business owners and solopreneurs who have stepped into this gooey emotional muck during the past few years of economic unpleasantness. Instead of lessons-learned and fuel for problem solving and innovation, setbacks are worn for all to see as Scarlet F's, where F stands for failure. Of course, what they forget is that no one can really see the Scarlet F's unless they go out of their way to project them through their attitudes.

You Own Your Attitude:

Striving not to fail is like walking up to take your turn at bat when the only thought running through your mind is, "don't strike out." The last two words, "strike out" are all that you remember as you flail wildly at everything thrown your way.

If you're caught up in an environment where an evil leader holds court, remember that you still own your attitude. While it's not easy to escape the fog of uncertainty and doubt created by these characters, it's unlikely that their attempts at mind control can survive in a pitched battle against your own good attitude.

If you are your own boss and you feel weighted down and exposed by the scarlet F's you believe you are carrying around with you, it's critical to rediscover the feelings of excitement, hope and opportunity that likely propelled you off on your own in the first place.

Rediscover or Reset Your Sense of Purpose:

Somewhere buried beneath the baggage and stress of the past few years, you had a sense of purpose that fueled your efforts. Whether it was providing for others or an intense desire to change the world, it's important to scrape off the muck and recall that sense of greater mission. Of course, we change over time, and what fueled us at one phase of life may not be so relevant at another stage. I know many people who have recharged their lives and their work as professionals by resetting their sense of purpose from a focus on success to an emphasis on making a difference for someone or some group.

The Bottom-Line for Now:

It's easy to focus on failure. It's a lot more fun, it's a lot healthier and it darned well is a lot more inspiring to rationalize our efforts and actions and combat our demons in the context of our bigger purpose.

Those who focus on success see victory around every corner. They view obstacles and setbacks as minor challenges to be overcome on a longer journey towards something worthwhile. No one can take away your sense of purpose, unless you let them. Focus your gaze clearly on the bigger picture and longer term, take a deep breath and then take the first step forward. You'll quickly remember that steps taken with a purpose in mind are effortless.

Now, keep moving.

Chapter 68

In Pursuit of Your Potential

You're good, but do you have it in you to be great?

I work with a lot of good professionals. These are smart people, all technically adept at their jobs and committed to working hard for their organizations. Only a few of these good individuals push themselves to become great.

Those that move from good to great are the driven ones. They're driven to learn, driven to push themselves, comfortable with trying and failing and well aware of the pearls of wisdom found underneath a nugget of gold buried in a pile of mud in every situation. They are looking, digging and diving for those pearls and nuggets.

Driven individuals are in competition, but it's not versus an external adversary. They are in competition with themselves. With resistance. With the temptation to take the easy route and be "just good enough."

I love working with these leaders. They are challenging and they are open to challenge. They've long since recognized the need to reflect and to gain feedback on their performance at every opportunity. They are relentless in pursuit of their own improvement.

I also recognize that not everyone is driven. That's OK. Just make certain if you're not driven, that you recognize the need to constantly tune your followership skills.

For those that sense there's more in you…that you want to leave it all out there on the field, perhaps you'll see yourself or, perhaps something here will kindle your flames of self-improvement.

Six Signs You Are Driven to Pursue Your Potential:

1. You understand that blocking and tackling are important. You're comfortable revisiting the basics of your profession. If it's leadership, you understand the need to revisit the purpose of your role and to continually strive to improve as a coach, as a mentor, a motivator and as a decision-maker.

2. You work hard to manage your own brand. While this sounds self-centered, it's actually socially intelligent. You recognize that your professional value proposition…the famous "Brand Called You" is all that you have and you work hard to see if the value proposition in your mind matches what others see in you.

3. You are genuinely interested in what others have to say. This natural tendency to seek the other person's point of view is more of that social intelligence and part of what makes you an authentic professional.

4. You are genuine in your dealings with others. Your internal values and principles match your external persona. You're in balance. A quote I read somewhere offered this as, "you believe what you say and you say what you believe."

5. You view power as the means to more. Not more money or fame, but rather the ability to produce more, to contribute more, to create more, to help more.

6. You recognize that success comes in many forms, but the best form is that internal sense of "I gave my best, there was nothing more." Of course, you always wonder whether there was just a little bit more in you to give.

The Bottom-Line for Now:

The life of a driven leader or a driven professional is filled with struggle and joy. Ironically, the joy is truly in the struggle. You just don't realize this until the struggle is over.

Chapter 69

Bad Bosses, Karma and Your Leadership Legacy

Thankfully, the human brain does a pretty good job of managing memories by helping us smooth out the bad times and enhance the good ones. This seems to work pretty well for a lot of things in life, with one major exception being our memories of lousy leaders we've encountered during our career.

Ask a room full of mid-level managers to talk about great leaders that have supported them and you get a few nice stories. Ask them for examples of bad leaders and bad leadership practices and you may have to run for high-ground as the trickle of mildly repressed memories turns into a torrent of frightening anecdotes described by individuals with a far-away look in their eyes and a tone tinged with revenge in their voices.

OK, I may be exaggerating a bit on the glazed eyes and revenge stuff, but not a bit on the ease with which people can describe being victimized by bad bosses. The stories of micromanaging, verbally abusive, backstabbing, credit taking, time-wasting bosses flow freely in these sessions, and are told with gusto. One story begets another and pretty soon, you have a room full of people trying to out do each other with, "you think that's bad, I had a manager that... ." Unfortunately, there's a lot of material for bad boss stories.

I've often imagined the poet Virgil and his counterpart, Dante, journeying through the Circles of Hell, only to come upon a special place reserved solely for the worst of the evil managers in our workplaces. I'll leave it to your imagination to work out what the appropriate punishment would be for these managers in this guaranteed blockbuster of a re-release of this literary classic. I can see the caption now: *Leadership Lessons from the Inferno!* Remember, you heard it here.

You Determine Your Own Legacy:

If you find yourself embarking on or immersed in a role in leading others, you have a choice to make about the impact you will have on those fortunate or unfortunate enough to serve with you. You can add to the inventory of "Bad Boss" stories by focusing on yourself, by not understanding what your true role is, and by doing everything possible to build your career on the backs of others. Or you can take the much harder, but ultimately, more rewarding path of doing the right things all of the time for the people in your care.

Eight Ideas for Building Your Positive Leadership Legacy:

1. Get to know the people who work for you. Your effort to pay attention and show genuine interest shows respect for your associates. Learn names, learn the names of their spouses and children, and pay attention to the pictures and personal mementos on their desks.

2. Listen more than you talk. You have two ears and one mouth...use them in proportion. Take the time for formal and informal discussions where you ask for input, feedback and ideas. And then do something with this input!

3. Dispense credit liberally. Never take credit that belongs to someone else. You are in the credit dispensing business!

4. Ensure that your actions match your words. We all know words are cheap. If you want people to commit to you and your vision, you've got to ensure that your "do matches your tell."

5. Know when to stay out of the way. If you've done your job picking the best people, creating the right working atmosphere and providing general direction, it's time to get out of the way and let people show you what they can do.

6. Enforce accountability. Everyone respects accountability. Enforce it fairly, evenly and consistently. No exceptions.

7. When things get tough, look in the mirror and point. The only finger pointing you should ever do is at yourself. Back your people, recognize that you are responsible for their results and if the results come up short, it is your fault, not theirs.

8. Keep your agenda visible. People sense when someone has a different or personal agenda. Don't let this be an issue. Your agenda is your team's success.

The Bottom-Line for Now:

Every time I feel like we're making some headway on stamping out bad bosses, I run into another group of great professionals who remind me that too many of our managerial experiences are lousy. Effective managers and leaders are made one person at a time, and every one of us makes a choice every day to do it right or not. What will your legacy be?

Chapter 70
Don't Let Your Self-Confidence Burn Out of Control

Self-confidence is rocket fuel for leaders. Used carefully and ignited under the proper conditions, it propels you and those around you to remarkable heights. However, beware the narrow tolerance ranges of your own self-confidence. Too little and you act and are perceived as weak. Too much and self-confidence becomes that most destructive of all leadership attributes, hubris.

In my experience, early career and first-time leaders tend to lack self-confidence, generally because they've not walked down the path and experienced the many pitfalls and challenges of the seasoned leader. Leadership self-confidence is born of experience, and not bestowed by title.

Some early leaders compensate with a command and control style, much like the parent who responds to her child with the self-serving and wholly ineffective explanation of "Because I said so," to the teenager looking for some rational reason as to why he should change his behavior. I'll let those of you with parenting experience highlight why this approach is doomed to fail.

Fortunately, as we gain experience, our self-confidence grows and many leaders leave their early career bad habits behind. Unfortunately, as time passes, a new potential problem often emerges. Confidence begets hubris, and hubris is only a short step away from arrogance.

Experience and Success Can Turn Self-Confidence to Hubris. Watch Out!

Jim Collins writing in his book, *"How the Mighty Fall,"* offers, "dating back to ancient Greece, the concept of hubris is defined as excessive pride that brings down a hero, or alternatively, …outrageous arrogance that inflicts suffering upon the innocent."

Perhaps it's human nature, but as we gain experience and enjoy some victories, it is easy to start believing we can do no wrong. This false and dangerous belief is often reinforced by the distorted reactions on our own performance that we receive from those who report to us. It's amazing how quick people are to tell us that we are brilliant when we're in charge.

When self-confidence moves out of tolerance towards hubris and arrogance, the fuel that propelled teams and organizations begins to burn in the working environment, distorting reality and destroying objectivity. The hubris of leaders is the accelerant that once ignited leads to the collapse of careers and companies.

How to Keep Your Self Confidence Within Tolerance:

- Remind yourself daily of your role as a leader. You are there to support, provide help, guidance, coaching and to create an environment for others to succeed in their roles.

- Live Deming's 8th point: *"Drive out fear."* You want to create trust and create a climate for innovation.

- Focus your calendar time on tasks that support the prosecution of your role.

- Remind yourself that leading is not about you. It's about everyone else around you.

- Ask people what you can do to help them succeed. And then do it.

The Bottom-Line for Now:

It's dangerously easy to start believing that *"you"* are the reason for your team's or your firm's successes. Once you buy into your own public relations, you're headed for a dangerous fall. Keep your edge sharp by focusing on what you can do to help others succeed…not on what they can do to once again prove how great of a leader you are. At the end of the day, you need enough self-confidence to know that the only way to create and sustain success is to choose carefully, support relentlessly and then place your trust in others.

Chapter 71

Dare to Be Different if You Dare

Greatness as a leader is earned by those willing to take risks for the right reasons.

It's good to be a good leader, so don't misconstrue the message in this essay. The world needs more individuals who care enough to consistently execute the blocking and tackling required to pass for effective leadership. My point here is that good isn't good enough, when the potential to be great at this activity that we call leading is within reach. Often, the distance of the reach to "great" is slightly beyond the cultural norms and leadership habits of your firm, so, it's up to you to stretch yourself that much further.

Let's back up for a second. If there were such a creature as a Leadership Anthropologist that spent his/her time studying the leadership development rituals and practices inside these closed ecosystems we call organizations, I suspect that one of the consistent observations would focus on the impact that the alpha-managers have on the development of the overall leadership culture. The observation might even be labeled as "Mimicry."

The top leaders of a firm directly impact the prevailing leadership culture through their own practices and their attention (or lack thereof) to the tasks of identifying and supporting the development of talent.

Show me a firm where the top executives engage with employees, talk openly about tough performance and organizational issues and focus on genuinely supporting talent development, and you'll more than likely find managers at all strata acting in similar fashion. Alternatively, spend some time at a safe distance observing the rituals of top leaders in firms that are otherwise focused on the transactional issues of day-to-day business and that rule with an imperial mentality, and you will likely observe that the rest of the tribe focuses on these transactional issues as well. The people-development tasks are reduced to simple, empty routines, including the often banal and inane annual performance review programs.

While too many leaders and too many firms focus on the short-term, transactional issues and leave the heavy lifting of talent development until some never-to-be-reached tomorrow, there are (thankfully) some conscientious individuals who understand the importance of their development and coaching activities. And while these individuals intuitively understand the benefits of investing time in creating great leadership and great talent-development practices, they often find themselves struggling as outsiders and outliers. They often find little support beyond lip service for these important activities.

In one example, a conversation with a senior executive at a highly regarded firm went something like this: *"We're great at recruiting the talent. Heck, people in this industry want to work here. Unfortunately, once we get them here, spend the time to evaluate and place them into our very sophisticated talent evaluation system, there's nothing on the other side that pro-actively supports their development. They spend a few years, put in the time and then go off to richer development and career opportunities with our competitors. We're training the industry,"* he added.

Recognizing the folly of this cultural norm, this professional has taken it upon himself to serve as an informal mentor for many of the firm's recruits, volunteering precious schedule and personal time to help right a wrong and do his part to change the culture for the better. *"It's reached the point now where people seek me out based on reputation. I don't mind that and in fact, I feel like it is my unspoken, unwritten responsibility to do what I can to help our firm get better at the development tasks of leadership. It's been noticed, and some of my peers are following suit."*

This manager dares to be different and the efforts are making a difference. What about you? What are you doing that transcends the transactional culture of your firm to strengthen your leadership practices and perhaps to catalyze an evolution or revolution in your firm's practices?

Five Ideas for You to Dare to Be Great-If You Dare:

1. Trust your gut. Again, if you are here reading this, you already intuitively understand how important it is to step up your own and your firm's leadership practices. It's time to put your convictions to work.

2. Forget waiting for permission. And forget waiting for someone or some group to solve leadership problems with new programs. You don't need permission to innovate around your own leadership practices and there is no program that magically changes a culture. Great practices develop and spread one manager at a time.

3. Think and act like a quiet leadership rebel. The greatest leaders I've encountered have redefined the system over time instead of conforming to it. Ensure that your "rebellious activities" are focused on allowing people to better serve, support and to create value for customers and for the firm and you'll find that it's difficult to end up in trouble.

4. Let your results be your best recruiting efforts. Like the colleague above who is now widely sought after for mentoring help, or that particular leader in a firm that everyone wants to work for, your consistent and genuine commitment to pushing the envelope on practices while delivering results will be your best recruiting tool. You will gain converts from your peers. Not all, but some.

5. Once results are visible, draw the "establishment" into your activities by asking for help. You don't need help, but it's amazing how much support you get when you appeal to someone's expertise. A conscientious executive team or HR group will jump at the opportunity to help you formalize a program that shows the ability to make a difference in a firm's effectiveness. The difference here is that you didn't go to them to ask for a program from scratch. You went to them with results and asked for help strengthening and formalizing.

The Bottom-Line for Now:

Daring to be different is not without some potential pain and cost. Most revolutions and revolutionaries face resistance and take casualties. Only you can decide whether you are comfortable putting yourself on the line. It's much safer to conform. The only cost of conforming is your leadership soul.

Chapter 72

Resistance and the Leader

It's no secret what's keeping you from achieving your goals. It's resistance.

Author Steven Pressfield does a masterful job in his short, powerful book, *"The War of Art,"* defining and then describing how to combat *resistance,* a powerful and vexing force of human nature that we might most often describe as procrastination. This book should be mandatory once a year reading for anyone over the age of ten.

Pressfield defines resistance as, *"...that destructive force inside human nature that rises whenever we consider a tough, long-term course of action that might do for us or others something that's actually good."*

Resistance shows up in many forms in our daily lives. It's what keeps us from eating properly, working out regularly and from taking that leap into a new job we've been dreaming about for years. Resistance pushes off to some unknown point in the future, the writing of the book that nearly everyone says they have in them. If none of those examples fit, think of something in your life that you know you should do, but haven't found the time or had the discipline to do it. That's resistance.

Resistance In the Workplace Takes On Many Forms:

- **Avoiding tough performance discussions.** "They're uncomfortable and maybe if we ignore them, they'll go away."

- **Focusing on the fire drills.** "We're swamped. I don't have time to think about the future."

- **Allowing the environment to govern your energy level and attitude.** "This place drains the life out of you. If they don't care, why should I?"

- **Silencing voices.** "I know we can do better, but my opinion doesn't carry any weight around here."

- **Resisting change.** "That's not the way we do it here. Every time someone suggests something different, they get shot down."

- **Bowing to bureaucracy.** "I just follow the company policy."

- **Not actively supporting the development of others.** "HR doesn't offer the training that we need."

Excuses! Of course, we're all human, and in my experience, even the most conscientious of leaders are capable of occasionally succumbing to the tyranny of resistance. I've observed good leaders grow a bit too comfortable with their teams and performance and almost unknowingly, they ratchet down their energy and intensity.

Those that are perceived as the strongest sometimes struggle very deeply with their own resistance. A retired CEO described to me that his biggest regret was never having the courage to conduct the tough discussions with his executives. He wondered how much his inaction in this area might have costs his companies over his career.

Six Ideas for Overcoming Resistance as a Leader:

1. Go back to basics. Revisit the core definition of your role as a leader. If your priorities aren't about creating an effective working environment, supporting others to achieve their objectives and supporting others to grow and develop in their careers, you need to redefine your role.

2. Assess: what is keeping you from acting on your core priorities? Is it like a diet, where you rationalize that it's OK to cheat, because you'll run an extra lap later? Or do you genuinely need some help, mentoring, training or guidance to develop the skill needed to execute on your priority?

3. Analyze your calendar. Eliminate as many "status update" meetings on your calendar and see if anyone notices. Fill that time with one-on-one and in-group discussions about topics that involve improving, growing, developing, innovating or doing anything other than talking about the darned status.

4. Become your own personal quality improvement project. Seriously. Define your own personal improvement project, and measure and track your performance on doing the things you've historically avoided. This is a powerful approach for those that benefit from measures and rigor.

5. Change your routine to combat resistance. Develop a routine that helps push resistance out of time and space. I write at a certain time every day, and I force myself to ignore phone calls, e-mails, tweets and fire alarms until the post is completed. Dedicate lunches to talking with your team members or block out calendar time to do nothing other than focus on development and coaching.

6. Use the buddy system. Find a similarly motivated peer and hold each other accountable. I do this with a colleague of mine and we push each other.

Just the knowledge that I would have to listen to him give me grief if I drop the ball on something that I've committed to, is enough to help me overcome my own resistance.

The Bottom-Line for Now:

Whether you call it resistance, procrastination or just plain laziness, the outcomes are the same. Nothing.

Overcoming resistance requires more than a slogan, a certain brand of fitness shoes and a sports drink. If you are conscientious enough to be reading the essays in this book, you are capable of identifying and defeating your sources of resistance. You might start with reading Pressfield's book as a source of inspiration. That is, if you can overcome the resistance that so often keeps us from cracking the cover and results in a stack of things that you plan on reading someday.

It's time to recognize the enemy of your progress and start taking action. Resistance hates action, and once in motion, action wins every time.

Chapter 73
Lead with Passion Every Day!

The passion a leader brings to his or her work is the secret sauce in a winning recipe for creating an effective working environment and developing a high performance team.

I had the good fortune recently to deliver a program on leadership to a group of technical professionals. These individuals were what I describe affectionately as "Data Geeks." These are professionals responsible for doing remarkable things with vast quantities of data. And while you're to be excused if you think that a program on leadership and developing as a senior contributor might not hold much attraction for this type of audience, the professionals that had the courage to sign up and attend this soft skills program wowed me! I was genuinely impressed with their enthusiasm and passion for their own development and their concern for the development of their colleagues.

The Power of Passion in the Workplace:

The passion a leader brings to his or her work is the secret sauce in a winning recipe for creating an effective working environment and developing a high performance team. Good leaders understand their role, work hard on developing their professional credibility, listen and ask questions and provide coaching and mentoring. Great leaders do all of the above, AND they infuse everyone around them with a sense of excitement for the adventure.

Jack Welch, in his book *Winning,* indicates, "Leaders make sure that people not only see the vision, they live it and breathe it." The best leaders do this by using their genuine passion and enthusiasm for their professional pursuits to help turn the working world and all of its inherent headaches and challenges into something that feels a lot like a great adventure.

Think about those managers you worked for who were marking time. They lacked passion for their work and for the work of the team, and I'll wager a cup of your favorite coffee their lack of passion was contagious. Thoughts of drudgery, boredom, compliance and visions of escape jump to mind when I think of the manager that was clearly just marking time and cashing a paycheck.

Alternatively, when I've been on teams where the leader was fully committed in words and actions to the team's success, and where challenges were viewed as future victories, the experiences and the results were remarkable.

Keep in mind that passion is different than disingenuous cheerleading. False praise and less-than heartfelt encouragement will only send people running in the opposite direction. The passion you show must reflect the pride you have in your team.

The Bottom-Line for Now:

It's never too late to rediscover a sense of pride and ownership in your craft. Remember, your attitude sets the tone for the work going on around you. Is this the week that you relight the pilot of passion in your work and help your team develop that sense of adventure that is so powerful for all of us?

Chapter 74
Engage with Purpose

Warning, this essay has been rated "I" for Intense by the Leadership Writers Association due to graphic intensity, strong and slightly colorful language and frequent cajoling to get it in gear and get moving. It's also been rated "M" for excessive Comingling of Metaphors in an attempt to make a point.

A fair number of leaders that I encounter are busy floating along on the current created by the urgent daily events in the workplace. This never-ending flow of "stuff to do" numbs their leadership senses and dulls their performance edges as weeks and months and quarters give way to more weeks, months and quarters. It's like sitting in the leadership equivalent of a lazy river at the local water park.

It's time to quit doing everything and getting nothing important done in the process. The best leaders that I know refuse to let the daily flow of activities derail them from their primary mission of driving results by helping people drive results.

These performance-focused leaders are intense. They engage with a purpose and view every encounter with an employee or a team as an opportunity to learn, to evaluate, to teach and to improve.

You know these characters. They are the ones that get things done and leave their people stronger and smarter in the process. They are also the ones that all of the motivated people want to work for in an organization. While they may not exude warmth or encourage group hugs, they do exude a sense of caring for the people that strive, learn and push the envelope on performance.

One of the keys to becoming a performance-focused leader is to master the art of asking the right questions. Constantly. These leaders engage with a purpose and maintain a high Questions-to-Comments ratio at all times. This high ratio allows them to learn, evaluate and identify opportunities to teach all at the same time.

Remember, they seek to understand, evaluate, teach and ultimately, to impact performance.

To understand a performance-focused leader and why he or she is constantly asking questions, you need to understand the questions running through their minds as they engage with you and your team members.

- How does this issue tie to our strategy?

- Does it change anything?

- Does it offer new options?

- How hard and how thoroughly has this individual thought through the issue at hand?

- Has he/she connected the issue to our strategy?

- How complete is the proposed solution?

- How can I coach this person?

- Is there real-time feedback to offer here?

- Is there a coachable opportunity?

- Is this individual earning my trust and the trust of teammates?

- Have my repeated encounters with this person raised a red flag?

- Have I just learned something that I did not know?

And many more.

One performance-focused leader described her every encounter with her colleagues as an opportunity to determine whether she was doing her job. "If they have a good grasp of the situation and have a well-developed idea or solution that aligns with our core strategies, then I've done something right. If the individual is weak in any of those areas, then I've failed to educate and support properly and chances are, others are struggling with the same lack of knowledge or insight. That's a sign that I need to step it up."

And while this intense, performance-focused leader might sound like a passionless automaton…a Leadership Terminator, they've simply learned to engage with a purpose without being jerks.

Five Suggestions for Improving Your Ability to Engage with Purpose:

1. Recognize the "Lazy River" syndrome that dominates our days. It usually starts with our willful submission to the tyranny of the calendar. We allow our days to be filled with meaningless chatter in endless meetings where people debate trivial nuances instead of hard issues. Regain control of your calendar and fill it with activities that focus on the right priorities. Or don't fill it all. Leave it open enough to engage and observe your people and teams in all varieties of settings.

2. Set the right priorities. They include items that deal with creating value, building competitive advantage, innovating and winning. Assess your own priorities and the priorities of your team members by attempting to connect activities to value creation with no more than one or two degrees of separation.

3. Teach your team members the questions that you want them to ask as they fight through their days. Does this fit? Is it a priority? Can I see how it either creates value or will help someone create value? Teach them your questions.

4. Ask the same questions at every encounter. People will learn what's important. Do something with what you learn from asking the right questions. See also the memo that says your priority is to drive results by helping people drive results. Start helping more and being an obstacle less.

5. Resist the "results at all costs" temptation. While this entire post is about driving results, as soon as you cross the white line of effective, people-focused, respectful, professional leadership practices and enter the "ends justifies the means zone," you've sold your leadership soul. Don't go there.

The Bottom-Line for Now:

Time is precious and leading is a privilege. No one can afford to squander either the time or the privilege that they've been entrusted to execute. Walk in the door with a sense of purpose. Create and instill this sense of purpose in the people around you and drain the water out of the Leadership Lazy River. You and your team can do better. Today.

Section 10
The Lighter Side of Leadership Caffeine

Before you get your hopes up too high, let the record reflect that I make no claim that I am capable of consciously writing anything that makes people laugh. However, a number of my posts managed to tickle the funny bones of my readers, and it seems appropriate to try and add something from the lighter side after enduring what must seem like 100,000 or so relatively serious essays, each incorporating at least seven suggestions for you to act upon. And while there might be a few lighter moments in the following pages, they are all presented in the context of a highly relevant message.

Enjoy my essays from, *The Lighter Side*. And if you happen to be recruiting comedy writers, please don't call! I'll stick to the mostly serious stuff.

Chapter 75

A Mostly Thoughtful Guide to Surviving Really Bad Leadership Days

Even the most dedicated and experienced of leaders will admit that there are more than a few days when they wonder whether it might not be a lot less stressful to hang up their leadership cleats in favor of an individual contributor role.

L ike marriage, not every day as a leader is filled with wine and roses. There are many days when you will drive home from work wondering whether you truly accomplished anything, and others when you will feel like you just took a few steps in the wrong direction.

Consider These Less Than Joyous Leadership Occasions:

- One of your top players and someone whom you've invested a great deal of time mentoring announces she is resigning.

- You just spent most of your day justifying your team's existence to upper management.

- In spite of knowing better, you lost it and snapped at someone that truly didn't deserve that reaction. (No one deserves that reaction.)

- You spent the day deciding who gets laid off and who doesn't.

- One of your team's major projects blew up and you spent the day as a human shield while your group took shots from everywhere in the organization.

- Your 360-degree feedback suggested that you have more than a few opportunities to improve.

- Speaking of feedback, you managed to end up with two people crying in your office today. You thought about it yourself.

- At 8:00 a.m., you saw the competitor's announcement of the game-changing new product. You suspect that your deodorant failed by 11:00 a.m. when you were explaining to the executives yet again, why you didn't have a good response to the competitor.

A Few Not So Serious Suggestions for Surviving the Toughest Leadership Days:

Start by reminding yourself of two key points:

1. What doesn't kill you makes you stronger.

2. Cannibalism is outlawed in most countries, and it is unlikely that you will be roasted and consumed. Since it cannot get much worse than that, consider yourself lucky and keep moving forward.

If points 1 and 2 above fail to assuage your anxiety, throw in the clincher of, "This too shall pass" and get back to work. Take solace in the fact that someday you will be upper management and then people will see what it's really like to walk on hot coals.

And Now for the Serious Side of Surviving the Toughest Leadership Days:

- Every problem or crisis is an opportunity to build your leadership skills, confidence and credibility.

- Problems create great learning opportunities. Don't waste these opportunities.

- It's the challenges that you and your team conquered that you will remember. Make some memories!

- Remember, you don't have to carry the weight of the world on your shoulders. If you've done your job and earned respect, your team members are there to help ease the burden. Ask for help.

- People aren't programmed to act and respond in ways that always fit your plans. Losing a great employee is painful, but if it has to happen, ensure that relationship transitions to one of valued and always welcome alum.

- Be thankful for feedback that says you can improve. At least someone cares.

- Leaders earn dividends over the long term. Your payoff comes a decade from now when the people that you are leading today are rising to new heights in their careers. They did the work but perhaps you played a small role along the way. Take pride in their accomplishments.

The Bottom-Line for Now:

There are no silver bullets for the bad days. They are inevitable and the best thing that you can do is stand strong against the fury and live to work and fix and build another day. The bad days remind you that you are human and not invincible, and they help balance out the days when you mistakenly start believing that as a leader you can do no wrong. Enjoy them all, for days, good or bad, are all that we have.

Chapter 76

The Cure for Tired Leader Syndrome

If only there were a pill to cure Tired Leader Syndrome!

I f the drug companies can do it, so can I. Pack together an entire host of symptoms, name a syndrome and produce the cure. Of course, the difference between my cure and what we hear on our televisions is that my side effects aren't worse than the actual problems.

Here's the Commercial:

Announcer comes on asking: *Do these images look familiar?*

Cue the Visuals:

Scene 1: Various images of clearly demoralized workers shuffling through their work or being dressed down by the boss for their obvious poor results.

Scene 2: A group of employees huddled by the water cooler suddenly grow quiet and disperse as the boss walks by.

Scene 3: (hey, this one's been done before, kind of, but I'm borrowing it): Shift to a visual of a boss staring out his office window at a workplace clearly in a state of turmoil, and then move to a close-up to the boss's face with a single tear rolling down his cheek.

Cue the Announcer for Narrative Questions:

- *Are you a leader that's been in your job for a long time and suffering from the following feelings of discomfort and inadequacy?*
- *Are you more concerned about protecting your job than helping your team members?*
- *Do your team members stare at their hands or at the ground when you are talking with them? Is your primary motivation making certain that your turf is protected at any cost?*
- *Do you and your team show almost no signs of innovation, learning or improvement?*
- *Do the long-standing routines that you require of your team members exist solely to make your life easier?*
- *Do you find yourself wondering why the idiots on your team can't solve problems without your involvement?*
- *Do you regularly feel like shooting messengers as a response to receiving bad news?*
- *When you sit alone in your office, do you wonder what it would be like to truly be good at your job and enthused about your work?"*

Announcer (after a slight pause):

- *If you experience one or more of these symptoms and especially the last one, you might be suffering from Tired Leader Syndrome or TLS. Don't worry. You're not alone. This debilitating condition affects a high percentage of leaders that have been in the same role for too long.*

- *Left untreated, TLS is often fatal to your career as well as the careers of those in constant contact with you. However, now, thanks to the miracles of modern medicine and marketing working hand in hand, there's a cure for Tired Leader Syndrome. With our pill and your commitment along with a fortune in coaching and a genuine desire to improve, you too can wake up, smell the coffee and rediscover why leading is a privilege and a serious professional responsibility.*

- *Yes, you too can rediscover that your true role is about more than building and protecting your turf. You'll remember that you are in your role to serve and support others and to drive positive results for your organization.*

- *As part of the process, you will rediscover your passion for encouraging, coaching and motivating others and the great feeling that comes from seeing others succeed and grow in front of your eyes.*

- *You'll also rediscover what it's like to lead and work with people that respect you without fearing you. I know, it sounds ridiculous right now, but over time, you'll come to understand that this is possible.*

- *It's not easy to overcome years of bad habits and a final cure in the most severe cases might require shock therapy, including being fired and having to start over on the lowest rung of the ladder.*

Cue the Next Set of Images: scene shows happy workers, good constructive discussion and a smiling, supportive boss that is welcomed into group discussions around the water cooler.

Announcer (Again):

- *There are no guarantees and Tired Leader Syndrome is a serious condition. However, now, you can talk to your coach about this in complete privacy and if he or she deems you eligible, you can start on your prescription today and start down the road to recovery from Tired Leader Syndrome.*

Cue the Final Image: Boss looking out the window with a smile and look of satisfaction on his face.

New, Fast Talking Announcer:

- *Possible side effects include the recognition that you are not fit to lead, severe stomach cramping, hang nails, toe fungus and a serious loss of self-esteem. If symptoms worsen, see your doctor or leadership coach immediately.*

The Bottom-Line for Now:

There is no miracle cure and no pill for Tired Leader Syndrome other than the recognition that leadership is truly a privilege and that you owe it to yourself and everyone around you to stay fresh, focused and committed to the role. I've seen many good leaders grow tired and then wake up thanks to a new assignment, a new boss who helped revive their spirits or as a result of recovering from an illness or a job loss. I've also met more than a few who we're too tired mentally and lacked the resolve to wake up and start leading again.

For those who refuse to wake up, I wish you a quick retirement. For those willing to take on the fight to overcome the slings and arrows of corporate outrageousness and creeping TLS, you have my complete support and regular encouragement. Focus and hard work are the only miracle cures I've found to date.

Chapter 77

The Meeting to Decide Whether to Outsource the Call Center

While this is a mild exaggeration, based on the decisions coming out of some organizations, these meetings must truly happen. If you find yourself in the middle of one, perhaps it's time to try something new.

Executive One: *"The numbers are undeniable. The money we'll save by outsourcing the call center to (insert country where English is neither a primary or secondary language) will add a full percentage point to our earnings this year. The savings come from paying below poverty-level wages and instead of a building, we're giving the people Burner Phones and letting them work wherever they want."*

Executive Two: *"Has anyone thought about the customers?"*

Executive Three: *"Screw the customers. If they don't like the service, they can switch to one of our competitors. And we all know that our competitors do the same thing. We're just keeping up. I fully support this initiative."*

Executive Two: *"Won't this adversely impact our image?"*

Executive One: *"We've done extensive polling, and we project that our customer satisfaction ratings will move slightly from their current "Dissatisfied" to "Genuinely Pissed Off." We can live with that. This keeps us well ahead of our two competitors who have ratings of "Hate Beyond Comprehension. Heck, we might even pick up some customers if we market this right."*

CEO: *"Do the people in this call center speak English?"*

Executive One: *"Yes, a bit. But since our manuals are written in a combination of Kanji, Sanskrit and Pig Latin, the customers will feel relieved to connect with someone who they can partially understand."*

Executive One's Lackey: *"Don't forget, we've created a fail-safe system to reduce call volume. The phone menu is a lot like playing "Angry Birds" blindfolded, and we suspect that 40% of callers will never reach the level where they connect to a real person."*

Executive One: *"That's right, Lackey. Thanks for reminding us. This is actually part of our corporate "Educate America" program, where we encourage more people to think for themselves and solve their own problems. And if someone is really stumped on an issue they can always use Twitter to get help."*

CEO: *"Brilliant...I've been looking for a social media strategy and you just nailed it."*

CEO: *"One last question, who do I call if I have a problem with one of our products?"*

Executive One: *"No worries, we've got our best local engineers available on call to take questions from the executive group."*

CEO: *"Great! How fast can we get this started?"*

The Bottom-Line for Now:

To all of the Executive One's and CEO's who perpetrate these miserable systems and services on customers, in my most disrespectful term, you are complete asses. If Dante were writing his Diving Comedy today, there would be a special level of hell reserved just for you. I suspect it would involve a miserable support call where you never get the answer, lasting for what seems like eternity. After all, that's what you do to us.

Get a clue. Respect your customers. Put the support help in the market you are doing business in...and if that happens to be here in America, hire, train and support some Americans. I for one am tired of the crap you pass off for support.

As for you geniuses who have decided that live support is only at the end of an instant message, your level in hell is currently under construction.

Chapter 78

Opposite Day and Other Ideas for Getting Unstuck

The best defense against a run of bad fortune is to unclench your jaw, take a few deep breaths and just smile. And then, keep moving. However, you might want to do the opposite of what you've been doing just to mix things up a bit.

I spend a great deal of time talking with you about driving change. We're forever prattling on about developing leaders, developing ourselves, developing strategies that hunt and generally living at the intersection of Noble and Pursuit. To heck with that (for today). Let's focus on where the rubber meets the road or our posteriors meet our desk chairs and contribute some ideas that will help us energize our teams, create a bit more energy and maybe, just maybe, send us back tomorrow towards Noble and Pursuit to resume our journeys.

Several Ideas of Varying Quality to Mix Things Up and Energize Yourself and Your Team:

1. Day filled with meetings? Show up early and remove the chairs from the conference room. Don't spend anytime explaining why you did this.

Conduct your meetings with a renewed sense of energy and enjoy the benefits of oxygen flowing freely to the brains in the room.

2. Need a personal change? Drive your spouse's car to work, park somewhere far away from your usual spot and walk to your desk a different way.

3. Continue your "day of different" by changing as many parts of your normal routine as possible.

4. Turn on your senses. Feeling like you're just moving blindly through your days? When you get to work, try and remember to write down 10 items or landmarks that you pass every day during your commute. Add 2 items per day for a week to this list.

5. Turn on your senses, part 2. Without cheating, write down your company's mission, vision and values statements. At last count, only 4 people in the western hemisphere were capable of completing this exercise accurately. Do this for several days and once you get them, start working them into office conversations. Observe how your co-workers react.

6. Cancel 50% of your meetings and try to fill the time with things you've been meaning to do. See if anything dire happens by not attending those meetings.

7. Plan ahead. Schedule customer visits and instead of a talking head trip, try to work it out with your customer where you will be able to see and hear from the people that use your offerings in their natural setting. Yes, this is a bit of social anthropology. Fire up those powers of observation and look/listen for problems and ideas. Compare notes with team members when you get back and vote on the top three items to pursue.

8. Invoke George Castanza and declare it opposite day. This famous character on the Seinfeld sitcom discovered that he was truly brilliant only when he would do the exact opposite of what he would normally do.

While this one may prove a bit risky, start small. Change up your lunch choice. When people ask for decisions, suggest that they make them on their own. If you would normally chair an ops meeting, delegate it to someone else. Skip the brainstorming session and let your team run through it. If you think that social media is a waste of time, ask a group to come up with ideas for using it to compete. If you are used to asking the boss for permission for everything, skip this a few times and just do the work. (Dedicated Seinfeld viewers may recall that George also found another way to dramatically increase his IQ. He gave up amorous activities. I'm not ready to suggest that one for you at this time, but if you fail to find something creative from this listing, it's next up in the batter's box.)

The Bottom-Line for Now:

One of my favorite signs in a great bakery in Mt. Prospect, IL reads, "Life is short, eat dessert first." While we are all part of some form of regimen in our work and in our lives, there are ample opportunities to mix things up, get the oxygen and blood flowing and add some creativity and fun into our days.

Chapter 79

Never Rake Leaves Uphill
& Other Management Lessons
Learned in the North Woods

Spend enough time writing, speaking and thinking about management and performance, and you're likely to find yourself looking for lessons in all of your dealings. This certainly held true for me this past weekend, as I engaged in the annual fall ritual of cleaning up the leaves at the north woods home.

While the management guidance here might not make the next issue of HBR, if you ever face several hilly acres of ankle deep leaves, this might just save your back from breaking!

First and foremost, never rake leaves uphill. Ditto for raking against the wind! Gravity and other forces of nature are your friends here. Don't fight them. Leaves tend to fall downhill, blow downhill and generally migrate towards their friends at low points in the land. Adding a little science (a very little!), you might reasonably conclude that the energy consumed per unit of leaves raked is pretty high when you push the little buggers uphill one at a time. Your goal here is minimal energy consumption on this task. Remember, after the leaves are gone, you've probably got to split a cord of wood.

In the Workplace: Too many projects feel a lot like raking leaves uphill. Poor project design and improper training result in a lot of commotion and little forward progress. And small obstacles easily become gigantic bottlenecks that soak up valuable management time and impact schedules and performance. If you feel like you are "raking uphill and against the wind," stop, assess and address the challenge from a new perspective.

On a personal note, if it is your wife that is raking uphill use your best tact and diplomacy to encourage her to rethink her approach. Trust me, I learned this one the hard way.

My second piece of north woods advice: Proper planning and flawless execution are required to effectively land a tarpaulin so that you can cover it in leaves on a windy day.

Anyone that has ever attempted to lay a tarp on the ground on a windy day understands the benefits of great teamwork and great team members operating in synchronicity towards a common goal. The same goes for challenging tasks and activities involving multiple team members in the workplace. It's easy to misfire and quickly become aggravated with poor performing or poorly trained team members, and then it's only a short step away from complete team meltdown. Take the time to clarify tasks, practice the execution and then provide team members with effective, real-time feedback.

Another personal note: if it's your wife or spouse that is misfiring on the tarp job, use your best tact and diplomacy to teach and encourage improved performance. Trust me, again!

Third: Don't ever plan on flying an airplane if you cannot consistently remember to raise the wheel on the leaf trailer before heading up your driveway. Every time I forget to do this, the trailer wheel digs a new ditch in the driveway and destroys another wheel.

In the workplace: risk management is a critical issue to be managed in real-time. Teach your team and yourself to constantly assess risks and build systems to identify and mitigate or eliminate those risks. Also, learn your limits. Some people and some teams just shouldn't fly airplanes or run nuclear power plants.

The Bottom-Line for Now:

May your fall clean up work be as filled with management and relationship lessons learned as mine!

Chapter 80

Beware Two-Dimensional Leader Disease

The burdens of leadership are pressing.

Just when you think you can't take on one more concern, you've heard about two new leadership illnesses from the Center for Leadership Disease Control here at Management Excellence.

A few essays ago, you were probably shocked to learn of the malady, Tired Leader Syndrome. After listening to the symptoms, you're convinced that you've got a bad case and you are desperately seeking a miracle cure. Something that involves no effort and that will quickly make this draining disease disappear. You've put a team on it and have people working around the clock to save your hide, but scientists and researchers hold out little help for chronic sufferers other than your complete and long-term isolation from anything that resembles a leadership role. You remain hopeful that your minions can save you.

Adding fuel to the fire was the recent announcement here at the Center for Leadership Disease and Control, that researchers have finally isolated the causes of a long-standing leadership wasting disease. This heretofore unnamed, but common set of symptoms is now called Two-Dimensional Leadership Disease or TDLD for short.

How Do You Know if You Suffer from Two-Dimensional Leadership Disease?

You could ask the people that work for you, but one of the first symptoms is that no one is comfortable sharing honest feedback about your performance with you. Too many messengers have been shot and too many impassioned pleas for you to start leading have gone unanswered.

One suggestion might be to eavesdrop or plant one of your minions into the populace to spy. You smile thinking about how brilliant you are to come up with ideas like that.

Another approach to self-diagnosing this odious wasting disease is to attempt to rally your team into one location and force them to physically raise their eyes from the ground or the table and look at you. It won't be easy to get compliance, but you can use a long-winded speech that emphasizes the glory of serving you in the name of the greater good of the firm. You'll probably draw upon an old favorite…berating someone weaker than you in public just to show that you're in charge. Certainly, this will make people look up to watch in wonderment as you masterfully use your power and position to reduce a former human being to a puddle of sweat. Finally, try making a few pleas to work harder, not smarter and then implore the team to look you in the eyes to see your fire and passion and to help them know that you are serious.

Once you've finally gained their attention, you should face forward, quickly turn around with your back to the group (a comfortable pose for you, since you're usually blocking out the credit for success that goes to the team), and then slowly turn sideways until you are standing at a 90 degree angle to the people in the room.

If you hear gasps of "Where did he go?" and "How did he do that?" and "Hey, he's finally vaporized himself, good riddance," then you know you've got Two Dimensional Leader Disease.

How do you know? You turned sideways and disappeared. As a leader, you have no depth!

The Bottom-Line for Now:

Add depth by remembering that you are there to serve, that it is never about you and that your success is directly related to how hard you work to support and promote and advance those around you. It's difficult to cure TDLD, but not impossible.

Chapter 81

My Ten Favorite Dumb
Ass Management Mistakes

Note from Art: this one is rated at least R for strong language.

Note 2: In the spirit of my post, "At Least 20 Things to Stop Doing as a Leader,"
I'm back with a list of some insanely stupid and all-too-common management
mistakes. These focus more on the decisions, actions or inactions that contribute
to creating even bigger problems. While I've remained on the positive side of the
law here (felons, you've had your day!), some of these mistakes are truly criminal.

My Ten Favorite Dumb Ass Management Mistakes:

1. Locking the corporate strategy in a drawer. Hey, I'm all for security, but this wasn't just protecting important documents. This executive didn't bother to share the strategy with employees either. It was a secret.

2. Not rolling out the sales compensation plan until late March. The sales team was on a calendar year. Hmmm, what did everyone do for Q1?

3. This one is epidemic...sucking the value out of an acquired company by folding, spindling, mutilating, disrespecting, vanquishing and

otherwise conquering and plundering the target. We've got a mountain of evidence of this, and still, dumb a@@ executives focus on the deal (the easy part) and forget the real work of properly and positively managing the new relative. Welcome to the family! Now bend over and cough.

4. Looking for cause in the effect. This is a daily occurrence in many businesses, where managers run around trying to explain the drivers behind company, competitor and market outcomes. "Hey, our competitor keeps putting up great numbers. They've gone to a formal dress code at the office. It must be the clothes." OK, that's a little far-fetched, but I double-dog dare you to find a few instances of misguided cause and effect in your workplace today.

5. Losing sight of the core issues in the heat of argument. The decision making process is complex. Add in a group of high powered and big ego managers and you're certain to be pressured into a dumb a** decision. My favorite evil tactic, "Take of your (insert function) hat and put on your business hat." You might as well have a lobotomy prior to making that decision, because that's what your evil counterpart is essentially asking you to do.

6. Letting marketing define its own key performance indicators. Hey, I'm a lifetime marketer, and I still rankle at this one. If the marketing activities don't specifically connect to the key levers that move the business forward, they are interesting to some, but useless to many.

7. Sliding down the slippery slope of consensus decision-making. Everybody doesn't get a vote unless we're talking about ordering pizza. We've all seen the cartoon that indicates in a series of panels what various functions are wanted in a new product development effort. The Rube Goldberg outcome looks nothing like what the customer wanted. Start looking for the moves away from smart and good in the consensus-based decisions on your teams. It should frighten you.

8. "We can't worry about what we've spent, we need to keep moving forward." Ha! This rationale has derailed careers and destabilized nations. For the love of all this is good in humanity, quit burning money when all the signs say "Stop!"

9. Daily occurrence in this economy: failing to acquire the right talent because of cost controls. Yeah, let's fix this one once we're making money! (For 20 bonus points, identify the insane and inane thought processes that went into that last statement.)

10. Annual occurrence: putting a group of managers in a room and expecting that out of the collective consciousness of this group, market winning strategies will emerge. "Hey, great meeting. See you next year." We'll maybe…unless our competitors leave us for global road kill.

The Bottom-Line for Now:

The common denominator in all ten of those very real mistakes is that they are controllable. We can decide to not make these mistakes. The sales comp plan can hit the street with the New Year. We don't have to throw good money after bad, and we don't have to engage in practices like the annual strategy planning retreat that are just stupid. If you can't go out and get the talent that you need now with what's walking around on the street, you're either not trying hard enough or you need to find some other people to work for.

Instead of thinking deep thoughts about making good decisions as part of your New Year's Resolutions, why not resolve to simply not make the same bad old decisions over and over again? Now that would be progress.

Epilogue

Since it is unlikely that many people will read this book in serial fashion from cover-to-cover, the demand for a parting note is somewhat minimized. Nonetheless, if you find yourself reading these words, I want to make certain they offer some parting guidance.

Every year during Thanksgiving week here in the U.S., I run my post, *"A Leader's List of Giving Thanks."* I've included it below, because it captures what I truly believe about the privilege that we have in supporting the development of others and in helping our organizations and businesses flourish and grow. Leadership is a privilege, and like any other privilege, it should be cared-for, protected and honored. And speaking of honor, it has been my honor to share time and ideas with you. It is my sincere hope that you found and continue to find many sparks of ideas that can help you grow, sustain and succeed in your professional and personal life.

A Leader's List of Giving Thanks

As we take a momentary time-out this Thanksgiving in America from our challenges as professionals, citizens and family members and give thanks for what's good and right in our world and lives, those of us that serve as leaders have a few additional reasons to be grateful for the opportunities that we have in support of others.

The Leader's List for Giving Thanks:

- Be grateful for your unique chance to serve others. It truly is a privilege.

- Be thankful for the patience and forbearance that your colleagues and team-members show as you learn over time and through trial and error what it truly means to lead.

- Give thanks for your chance to learn from others.

- Pay honor to those that came before you and took the time to pass along their wisdom…even if you didn't realize how valuable it was until much later.

- Be in awe of the opportunity that you have in front of you to positively impact lives in ways that few other jobs or professions provide.

- Be inspired to motivate, coach and teach those that invest valuable time in their lives and careers with you.

- Give thanks for the opportunity that you have to create value for your organization. You might not engineer new products or services, but the people that work for you enable others to perform their jobs creating or building or supporting at high levels.

- Be grateful that you were given or developed the patience to cope with the daily stresses and strains of leadership and to keep reminding yourself that it is all worth it in the end.

- Give thanks for your chance to participate in the journey of a lifetime.

- And most of all, just give thanks by speaking up and remembering that a well-placed, heartfelt "Thank you" is one of the most powerful and important of all leadership tools.

And yes, please accept my sincere Thank You for your readership and conversation. I am truly grateful for you.

-Art

Acknowledgements

While writing is a solo activity, no one truly writes alone.

- Bob Lindner, thanks for the idea! You started this one in motion. Thanks as well for providing remarkable web services…and for being a good friend.

- Sarah Sullivan, for regularly reminding me that I had committed to writing another book. (Thanks as well for your support for the first book!)

- Eric Lieberman, you offered encouragement and reminded me that the real writing takes place in the editing.

- To my many students, clients, seminar and keynote participants, thanks for letting me try my ideas on for size.

- To my wonderful friends in the leadership blogosphere who provide daily inspiration, thank you!

- Amber Wallor, it's likely I would have bailed on this somewhere in the depths of my self-doubt, without your unbridled enthusiasm, your repeated readings and your increasingly confident suggestions on what was working and what wasn't. And thank you for a cover design I truly love.

About the Author

Art Petty is an experienced senior executive bringing global marketing, sales and strategy capabilities to his employers and clients. He is the founder of Strategy & Management-Innovations, LLC where he serves small and mid-sized firms for strategy and marketing consulting and executives and developing leaders as a coach.

Art is the co-author of the book with Rich Petro, *Practical Lessons in Leadership*, and the author of the popular Management Excellence blog (http://artpetty.com) where he writes on a broad range of management and leadership topics.

In addition to consulting and training, Art is active as a business and management educator, serving as an adjunct faculty member at DePaul University in the MBA and undergraduate programs.

Art is married to his high school sweetheart and lives with his two sons and one cat in Crystal Lake, IL.

Made in the USA
Columbia, SC
24 May 2020